'Quartet'

(Sequel to Visions)

To

Bill

Best Wishes

'Quartet'

'I lived while you loved me'

Herbert Edgar

VIKI Books
Inverness. Florida

Publisher's note: This is a work of fiction. Names, characters, places and incidents have been used in a fictitious context. Any resemblance to actual persons, living or dead, is entirely coincidental.

First U.S. edition.

Library of Congress Catalog Card Number: 94-61943

Quartet : a novel by Herbert Edgar

ISBN 0-9640363-1-2

Published in the United States by: Viki Books
Inverness,
Florida 34451-1228.

Printed in the U.S.A. -- First edition: February 1994

Book design by Geoffrey Terry

'Quartet'

(Sequel to Visions)

Prologue

Il Palazzo Grassina was a grand edifice, consisting of forty-six bedrooms, several reception rooms, the great dining hall, the library and *'Il salotto'*, a huge sitting room.

On the west side, and connected to the main building by way of a covered passageway, stood the music room, which was lined with carved wood paneling, resulting in near perfect acoustics. An identical passageway, on the east side, adjoined the conservatory, an hexagonal glass building which housed a vast array of tropical plants, including a dazzling variety of orchids.

The entire structure dominated one of the velvet green hills of Tuscany and presented magnificent views of the splendid historic city of Florence and the Arno river.

Several acres around the palace were landscaped into a park-like setting, with massive oak trees, pines, poplars and an abundance of tall, rambling azaleas, that painted huge splashes of red, pink and orange each spring. Closer to the house, a profusion of plants in a harlequin of colours jostled for position in the flower borders.

Many limestone statues stood guard around the estate, as they had done for the past four centuries, and more recently a swimming pool had been added, giving no clue as to its contemporary origin and looking deceptively Roman.

Above all the cyprus trees, so powerful in their statement that 'this is Italy', lined the carriageway to the main gate and enhanced the architecture by their carefully considered positioning, complementing the immaculate design of the palace to perfection.

The sixteenth-century building had some special magic. Roberto's ancestors had invested more than money; they had incorporated the family heart, which had sustained a firm, constant beat uninterrupted throughout the centuries, in the name of Grassina.

Following the death of his father, just a few days before, Roberto had inherited title to the estate. He would in future be known as Baron Roberto Grassina.

The maid entered the room where Valerie still slept, and taking care not to disturb her, opened the heavy, gold embossed, brocade drapes, tying them back with large tasseled silk ropes.

Valerie's bedroom was one of the most beautiful in the house. A symphony of stone and handmade brick walls separating the mosaic floor, where cherubs and angels danced in vivid colour, from the vaulted ceiling. Everything was right, from the massive, carved oak door, perfectly balanced and defying the fact of its own weight, to the arched windows, five in all, facing east to permit the sun to greet the fortunate occupant of the room called *camera del est* (the east bedroom).

When Roberto kissed Valerie goodnight, in the early hours of the morning, he preceded her into the room with a candle. The flickering light played on the antique furniture that contrasted solid construction with fine and delicate carving.

They had known each other for only ten days and yet the intense passion they felt for one another could be tempered with no sense of hunger. Before parting, a gentle kiss satisfied them both, knowing as they did, it was a promise for the night of their wedding. They had agreed their bodies would not touch this night, they would deny themselves just once more. Thereafter there would be no inhibitions, or limitations.

Soon the warmth of the sun on Valerie's face caressed her to a gentle transcendence from sleep to wake. Slowly her eyelids permitted the passage of more and more light; golden light from the morning sun that flooded the room, filling every corner.

As her eyes became accustomed to the light she glanced around at the beauty Roberto had promised she would experience. It was now the turn of her mind. Yesterday had been a day so marvelous that, before commencing another, she wished to re-live every moment.

Valerie had spent a night at the palace previously, just a few days before, though on that occasion the circumstances had been in no way similar and it had been a different room that cradled her night of dreams.

Yesterday, Roberto's sister Claudia had introduced her fiance, Peter, and Valerie's mother to *Palazzo Grassina*. Both were enamored with the magnificence, grandeur and tranquility of the place.

Most of the relatives and guests who had been present, just two days before, for the funeral of the Baron, Roberto's father, had remained at the palace once the forthcoming double wedding had been announced.

Edoardo, Roberto's cousin, had, with great enthusiasm and proficiency, made all the arrangements and everything appeared, on the surface, to be calm and ready. A marquee had been erected on the lawn in front of the main entrance, its simple, stark construction masked by a mass of flowers both inside and out.

Valerie continued to reflect upon what had been the happiest day of her life. She snuggled once more into the comfort of the linen sheets, then stretched herself, breathing deeply the perfumed air from the flowers that filled her room.

Somehow, unknown to Valerie, Roberto had arranged with Edoardo that he drive to Switzerland and collect her mother. They were waiting at the airport in Florence when Valerie arrived with Roberto, Claudia and Peter, following their ten-day adventure together.

The family and friends at the palace had given the four an enthusiastic welcome, following which a barbecue dinner was held in the garden. As they ate, drank and laughed together an orchestra played traditional Neapolitan melodies.

That day had passed, though Valerie had wished it could last forever. The warmth of the people had completed her indoctrination and she now felt completely at home.

Another day was about to begin. Something she had not contemplated, she was to marry. Even four days previously there was no thought of such an event and yet, today, she was to take the vows that would make her Baroness Valerie Grassina, wife of one of the most important figures in Italian aristocracy.

Valerie was elegantly beautiful, with long, wavy, auburn hair, kind green eyes that had just a hint of brown and full lips. Her cheek bones were high and her body perfect; slim, firm and shapely.

For such an attractive woman to arrive at the age of twenty-seven without having been married or even engaged was a reflection of her intelligence. She had simply not met the right man and was not prepared to waste her life on the wrong one. There was no doubt in her mind where Roberto was concerned; when he suggested marriage she accepted instantly, there was no reason to delay.

Roberto had a similar history. He had been blind for the first thirty-one of his thirty-two years and had lived in a fantasy world of romance for two years prior to meeting Valerie, constantly dreaming of the same girl. He had pictured her so clearly in his mind that he had described her in a book, dictated to his sister Claudia. Once he met Valerie, under rather incredible circumstances, it was no longer necessary to dream. She was a manifestation of his fantasy.

The rejoicing at the palace had continued well into the early hours of the morning and the last things Valerie remembered, before retiring to her room, were the smell of honeysuckle and the warm air.

The hands on the beautiful *capo del monte* ceramic clock indicated 10 a.m., time to make an appearance, she thought. The wedding ceremony was not scheduled to take place until 3 p.m. However, from previous experience at a palace banquet Valerie could imagine what to expect at the wedding breakfast and determined to limit herself to a cup of coffee for breakast.

She opened the door of the bedroom and instantly her eyes met those of Roberto, where he sat across the corridor.

"Good morning, dearest Valerie."

"Roberto, good morning, how nice to see you. Have you been here long?"

"Just half an hour. I didn't want to disturb you. You know I find myself very curious to see how you react to everything and every situation." He took her arm and guided her along the corridor. "I love you, as you know, but it's much more than that. I love to see how you move, how your face lights up at the sight of something new. There is so much that fascinates me about you, I cannot explain. You must not be embarrassed if I seem to study you too much, I imagine it has to do with having been blind for thirty-one years. When I see something that gives me pleasure I am afraid to take my eyes from whatever it is in case that pleasure be suddenly denied me."

"I feel the same," Valerie responded, looking deeply into the eyes that had been dead for so long. "When I opened my eyes this morning I had a sensation I have not experienced since I was a child. The sort of feeling I remember from my very early Christmases, looking forward to opening the packages. In this case you are the package. I must tell you that the room and the view took my breath away when I awoke this morning. As you said, no artificial light could show the room as the sun did."

They embraced for a moment, then he led her to the summer room by the pool, where they had a breakfast of caviar and champagne, the resolve of coffee-only having been forgotten.

Both had rested comfortably and well but had hardly slept at all, their minds likewise consumed by thoughts of the day ahead. Now that day had arrived.

For a while they chatted happily together, then their conversation was disturbed by the arrival of Peter and Claudia who had returned from a tour of the palace and grounds. Peter had travelled extensively and had seen many beautiful places, including much of Italy, but he confessed he found *Palazzo Grassina* enchanting. Although it was a very large building, that was not the impression it gave. It blended into the countryside and belied its size with charm and elegance.

"Well, my friends, we have come through a great deal together," Roberto announced, "and now we are about to undertake the same major step in our lives. I am, by nature, a cautious person, however, I have never felt so confident of anything in my life as I feel concerning my faith in the three of you." All agreed that the feeling was mutual, "Let us drink a toast to our friendship. May I suggest naming ourselves Quartet?" Each had complete trust in the others and they swore an allegiance together for as long as they lived. Peter jokingly remarked, "Something like a mini NATO," and confirmed that he thought Quartet was an apt and all-embracing description of their relationship to one another.

Each had a warm feeling and felt very privileged at having *three* good friends. Such a rare situation justified what appeared to be a childish gesture.

Roberto filled four glasses with champagne and passed them around. They held the glasses high and in unison declared, "Quartet." There followed that unmistakable ting, the sound of crystal glasses striking; then each enjoyed the consumption of the sweet liquid, sealing the dedication.

It wasn't necessary to cut fingers and combine blood, but such a powerful feeling of friendship and trust deserved to be declared.

One

Following breakfast the Quartet went for their meeting with the Bishop to discuss the details of the wedding ceremony. Because the couples had decided to marry with such little notice the civil requirements would be completed after they returned from their honeymoons.

The arrangement was that there would be a religious ceremony in the chapel attached to the palace. The time factor made it convenient for the family, the majority of whom were pleased to remain on for the extra two days necessary.

It was only a few days since the Quartet passed through Brasov, in Rumania, at that time being given a lift by a German truck driver called Hans, who prompted their memory that Brasov was the town of Castle Bran and Dracula.

It would be an anticlimax, after so much excitement, to lie on the beach in the Bahamas or some such place; consequently they had decided Rumania would be an ideal location for their honeymoons, providing interest and intrigue. Brasov would be their destination.

They planned to leave for Rumania the next day and combine the opportunity to collect Peter's beloved Ferrari from Bucharest, following the repairs necessary when it had been damaged while being driven by a Rumanian secret service agent. The honeymoon would keep them away for three weeks.

Upon their return to Florence there would be the civil ceremony and the signing of the register. A little unorthodox but perfectly satisfactory. Subconsciously Roberto had decided on the unusual wedding arrangements as a method of stabilizing the family after the loss of his father.

Following the final confirmation of their vows the Quartet would begin their new lives together. Roberto, at the head of the family Grassina, with his wife Valerie and his dear sister Claudia, with her husband Peter.

Either couple would move into one of the gate houses on the estate. Thereafter their lives would be very closely linked, both in business and pleasure.

The east and west gate houses were just two kilometers apart, identical in design and luxuriously appointed; in fact, Roberto's father had devoted a great deal of energy to perfecting the structures and guiding the interior designer as to what he required.

It was for his two beloved children that he had lavished so much on the buildings, his dream being that one day they would take up residence there with their spouses, followed in time by his becoming a grandfather and seeing his grandchildren raised in the exquisite surroundings.

The Baron had been prepared for a long wait before his dream would be fulfilled, though he hoped it would occur during his lifetime. It was not to be. His life had been extinguished and now the weddings of both his offspring were about to take place in a much shorter time than he could ever have hoped or imagined.

Following their meeting with the Bishop, Claudia gained Valerie's attention.

"Come on, let's go up to my room. I have a surprise for you."

They went upstairs to the dressing room adjacent to Claudia's bedroom. In the middle of the floor stood two tailor's mannequins, each fitted with an identical wedding gown.

"Well, what do you think?" Claudia taunted, a very contented look on her face.

"They are magnificent," Valerie replied excitedly as she moved slowly around the display. "Classic, elegant and charming, but how did you manage to find them? I had expected to wear a two-piece suit." It was not just the beauty of the gown that intrigued Valerie, it was the fact that in such a short period of time so much had been achieved. Edoardo's meticulous attention to detail had encompassed even the unlikely detail of obtaining the wedding dresses for the girls, a totally unexpected and pleasant surprise for Valerie. Claudia had known of the arrangement and had suggested to Edoardo that they wear identical gowns, thus underlining the affinity that existed between them.

They agreed to help one another with their preparations and two of Claudia's aunts, Simonetta and Cecilia, insisted on providing their assistance.

The excitement began to increase with the momentum of activity around the palace. Every few moments there was a new delivery.

The flowers were already in position and the tables in the marquee were beginning to fill with the various sets of cutlery, and wine and champagne glasses. Guests had been coming and going all morning, bringing, on their return from Florence, some delightful or elegant gift for each of the couples.

An outside kitchen had been established and the air began to fill with the delicate aroma of herbs, while three chefs jostled for position at the wood-burning stoves and ovens.

An orchestra was rehearsing and many of the guests were singing with the orchestra.

Peter and Roberto returned from the stables and Valerie noticed that Roberto was limping rather more than he had been during the previous couple of days. The wound to his leg had been severe and it would probably be several weeks before it healed completely.

"Roberto, you have been overdoing it, you should sit for a while," Valerie whispered as Roberto took her hand and kissed her on the cheek.

"Don't worry, Dr. Fioruccio will be arriving soon. On the telephone last night he told me he wants to have a look at the leg. Well, come with me and help me dress. With your help I will be able to keep off my feet."

They left to go to Roberto's room while Claudia went with Peter, who was still bubbling with excitement at what he had seen since his arrival at the palace.

Valerie's mother revelled in the activity and was delighted that her daughter was about to be married to such a handsome and important man, although she continued to be frustrated by being unable to satisfy her curiosity completely concerning the previous ten days. She had heard the basic facts of the drama from Edoardo, as they drove from Switzerland, but the finer details were yet to be recounted; however, she knew she must wait. This day was Valerie's and the joy of the occasion was contagious, such a contrast to what had happened one year ago.

She had suffered so much for her daughter, crying almost continuously when they were not together, that such a beautiful girl should suddenly lose her sight. Thank God something that could have been permanent was reversed, just as suddenly, a little over one year later. While a victim of a train crash in the Black Forest, her sight miraculously returned following a severe blow to the head.

The anticipation of the ceremony touched all. It was right that the head of the family should have a wife. Before being fully aware of the circumstances surrounding the meeting of Roberto and Valerie, some of the older members of the family were indignant that she was not Italian, although their concern subsided once the full details of the preceding ten days were known. There was no one who would have things differently.

Claudia was highly respected by the entire family. It was she who had maintained the monthly newsletter in an endeavor to keep the family united and abreast of all the latest developments. Valerie had Claudia's stamp of approval and that was sufficient for most. The fact that she had almost certainly been instrumental in saving the life of Roberto, in the Czech Republic, convinced the most hard-headed.

It was fortunate indeed that both Peter and Valerie had been raised in the Catholic faith, consequently the service would unite both couples in the eyes of God. The laws of the city of Florence would be satisfied after three weeks.

The moment of the ceremony was drawing close and Edoardo was guiding the last few guests to their seats when his pager began to beep. He glanced down and saw that the telephone number indicated on the unit was that of his office.

His secretary had strict instructions that he was not to be disturbed this day except in the most extreme emergency; therefore, there was some serious problem. What could it be? he thought to himself. He called his two aunts, Simonetta and Cecilia, asking that they continue to seat the last few guests, then he left the marquee.

Edoardo hurried to the study in the main house rather concerned. He knew his secretary well enough that she would not disturb him unless it was absolutely necessary.

The number had hardly begun to ring when the soft voice of Loridana responded. She was waiting and anxious for his call.

"What is it, Cara?"

"There are some men here. They wa---." At that point the receiver was snatched from her. Then a strange voice began to speak clearly and without feeling.

"Signore, I have to tell you that there has been an accident, your wife and daughter have been killed."

"Who are you, what are you saying?"

"My name is not important, what is most important is that you come to your office immediately." At that point there was the click of the receiver being replaced and a signal indicating the line was dead.

Edoardo had very quick reactions that overruled his questioning mind. Questions like: what has happened, who are these people, and the shocking question, is it true that my wife and daughter have been killed? That was absurd, there was certainly some terrible mistake.

He leapt into action immediately. First he took a sheet of paper from the desk and scribbled a note for Roberto. Though he could not deliver the note, he knew Roberto well enough that he was sure he would leave the ceremony instantly to be at his side. He therefore sealed the note in an envelope, ran back to the marquee and handed it to Cecilia, instructing her to pass it to Roberto after the ceremony.

"Don't worry" he told her. "It's nothing serious but I have to go to the office immediately."

Cecilia smiled and tucked the envelope into her pocket. He probably has some surprise for the two couples, she thought. "How long will you be?" she queried.

"I don't know, but I will return as soon as possible."

Roberto's bedroom looked out onto the front drive and he was standing by the window with Valerie, contemplating the remarkable changes in their circumstances during the previous ten days, when Edoardo ran to his Alfa 164, which shortly accelerated out of the drive. Roberto drew Valerie's attention to what he saw.

"Valerie, my dear, I am afraid Edoardo has a problem. We must go downstairs and see what it's all about."

Roberto took Valerie's arm and they quickly made their way to the marquee and to Cecilia, who was showing two more of the guests to their seats. Cecilia would know what was going on.

"What is Edoardo's problem, Aunt Cecilia?"

"Oh, I was supposed to give you the note after the ceremony, he said it was nothing serious." As she spoke she took the envelope from her pocket and handed it to Roberto.

He read the short note and handed it back to Cecilia, instructing her to get it to Claudia as soon as possible, and as he redirected Valerie back out of the marquee he called back to Cecilia to ask the guests to be patient. He would telephone from Edoardo's office as soon as he knew what had happened.

Valerie felt she did not need to ask and she was right. Roberto began to tell her as they hurried to the garage.

"The note just said that Edoardo had to go to the office urgently. But I know my cousin. He would not miss this day unless it was something very serious."

"Can you not call him on the car phone?" Valerie asked.

"For some reason I think not, don't ask me why."

The BMW series 7 effortlessly negotiated the descending, winding road at the high speed Roberto maintained. Valerie felt no fear of the journey, though she was very apprehensive of what they might find when they arrived in Florence.

Somehow it seemed strange to her that she had no premonition of what was happening. Maybe she no longer had that extra vision that had served her so well during the previous ten days.

The power had come to her when it was needed even though when she became aware of it she had no idea of how to call upon it. She began to wonder how she could trigger the psychic ability she had inherited. Then she remembered she had had the feeling the power had died when she used the maximum force in France to put an end to the life of the wicked medium.

"What are you thinking about?" Roberto inquired.

"You remember when Massenet died and I told you I had been responsible for her death? I also said I thought the power had left me. I was just wondering if I could find some way to activate it once more. It would certainly be very useful at this moment."

"Don't worry, whatever the problem is we will sort it out. Well, here we are, these are the offices of the family business."

They had arrived at a very old, long, low building, constructed of a mixture of stone and handmade bricks in a random selection. Many buildings in Tuscany employed the same techniques. A series of arched windows ran the length of the building and upon each pane of glass lettering in gold indicated legal studios, banking, exchange facilities, etc.

"Where is Edoardo's car?" Valerie wondered.

"He probably drove to the car park area at the rear of the building. For us I thought it best that we park here. You had better remain in the car, I won't be long."

"Roberto, I really would prefer to come with you, I---" Suddenly she stopped speaking and seemed to freeze where she stood. Then she began to speak once more, this time in the strange monotonous tone that was quite foreign to her and that he had heard on a couple of occasions previously when the strange force seemed to take over. Roberto chilled at the sound of her voice.

"Behind the building there are four cars and nearby three men dressed in elegant black suits. Inside the building, in a very large room, Edoardo is sitting in a leather chair by a desk. He has his head resting on his hands and is crying. Beside him there are five other men dressed in black suits. The men are evil but they will not harm you. One moment, there is something on a long table. The image is not clear but I feel sure there are three bodies. Yes, it is becoming more clear now, there are bodies of two women and a man."

"So the visions have returned and just in time. The men you described are members of a vicious mafia group from Palermo."

Roberto took the handset from the car phone and quickly dialed a number. Following a short delay he began to speak calmly and precisely. He then replaced the receiver.

Roberto's face assumed a very serious look and he remained silent. She studied him. He was the first person she had seen when her sight returned, although at the time he was injured, lying in a pool of blood and in bad shape. It was obvious that he was very handsome; dark skin, thick, black, short curly hair, a black moustache, tall with broad shoulders and dark flashing eyes. The circumstances of that first encounter were so terrible and yet she felt love for him instantly, a fact that convinced her she had never been in love before. The sensation was something new, exhilarating and exciting, a feeling that struck deep in her heart.

Roberto and Valerie continued their silent vigil until, after approximately fifteen minutes, four limousines turned onto the road fifty yards in front of where the BMW was parked and slowly moved toward them. The vehicles came to a stop just in front of where they were waiting and as they did so Roberto began to walk toward the first car. Shortly four or five men from each car joined Roberto. Valerie recognized many of the faces from the wedding party. Peter was also amongst them.

Quickly the group broke up and began to move to the rear of the building in a staggered file.

Once out of view of the road Roberto and his group began to extract weapons from their jackets, some with revolvers, some with shot guns. They prepared for action.

Roberto, still at the head of the group, lowered himself to a crouched position and slowly and carefully peered round the corner. As Valerie had said, there were in fact three men dressed in black; however, none was armed. Roberto whispered some instructions to the men nearest to him. They appeared not to agree with what he said. Roberto assumed a look of authority, then the men nodded in agreement.

Roberto slipped his pistol back into his jacket pocket, then slowly stepped forward with his hands above his head. There was a short delay, then Roberto called out some instructions, following which, slowly, the other men also pocketed their weapons and began to move forward.

Two

Around a massive, oak conference table sat a group of very grim-faced men dressed in black suits. On the table lay three lifeless figures, the bodies of a young man, a young woman, and a girl, wearing swimming costumes.

At the head of the table, Edoardo sat with his head in his hands, sobbing bitterly. His heart still beat, he was breathing but his life was finished. The only woman he had ever loved and his beloved daughter could respond to him no more. His eyes could no longer revel in their lives. A strong-willed and strong-bodied man of honor and dignity had collapsed within.

Soon the file, headed by Roberto, entered the room accompanied by a further figure dressed in black. The unexpected scene that greeted the new arrivals stunned each and every one.

Outside in the car Valerie sensed the tragedy and decided that despite Roberto's instructions she must now join him. She got out of the car and began to walk toward the building. Then, from one of the other cars, she saw Claudia hurriedly walking toward her. When they met Valerie was visibly shaking and her face deathly white as she stated somberly, "Claudia, I am very concerned, something terrible has happened. The pictures that are trying to manifest in my mind I don't want to see or believe. I am going in there. Will you come with me?"

"Of course, come on, let's go." Claudia and Valerie followed the route previously taken by the men and as they entered the room Roberto and Peter met them. Anticipating their reaction at the sight of the bodies on the table, they took the girls' hands and felt the shock and horror that filled them both.

Claudia glanced at the group of men around the table, recognizing them as Don Carini and his bodyguards, "What the hell are they doing here?" she snapped.

Roberto cautioned her to be calm and indicated where Edoardo remained unmoved by the arrival of Valerie and Claudia.

Don Carini stood, then slowly and quietly began to speak, addressing everyone but looking directly at Roberto.

"The Carini family extend to you and your family their most sincere condolences on the deaths of Eleanora and Gina."

Having made that brief statement he instructed his men to leave the room. Then he turned once more to Roberto and suggested that those remaining should sit around the table to discuss what had happened.

Roberto introduced Valerie and Peter, then everyone took their seats as Don Carini began to speak once more.

"I knew of the weddings that were to take place today and I'm sorry your plans have been disturbed by such a terrible tragedy."

Roberto walked around the table to where Edoardo sat, placed his arm on the shoulder of his cousin and whispered,

"Please try to calm yourself, dear cousin. It is imperative we discover the full circumstances of what has happened."

Edoardo raised his head, wiped the tears from his eyes and acknowledged Roberto's suggestion with a nod of his head, then after a few seconds of silence said, "I will be all right, please continue."

Don Carini turned his eyes in the direction of the young man on the table and said, with a trembling voice,

"He was my son. His name was Giulio. Yes, today I have lost my son, my daughter, and my grand-daughter. It is no longer possible for me to keep the secret. I must now bring shame upon myself and my family."

Valerie looked hard at Don Carini. She knew for sure he was an evil man with blood on his hands, nevertheless he was a man of certain principles. Her continued visual assessment was interrupted as Carini continued after a brief pause,

"When my good wife, Anna, was pregnant with our beloved daughter Eleanora, I was for one night, and one night only, away from home. I shall curse that night forever. I had to meet a new and very important business client. The meeting was scheduled to take place at an hotel in Rome. In those days I followed the orders of my father and because of secrecy the only instruction I was given was that I should go to room 311 at the hotel. I was not given the identity of the person I was to meet." Carini took a deep breath, the confession he was in the process of making represented the most painful experience of his life. "I excused myself to Anna and told her that I would probably remain at the hotel overnight."

Roberto and Claudia had never before heard Don Carini speak in this manner. They knew him only as a despicable mafia boss.

"On arrival at the hotel I made my way to room 311, as instructed, and knocked on the door. When the door opened I was surprised to be greeted by a beautiful young woman. She invited me in and we conducted our business. During the course of the evening, dinner was brought to the room and later, when our business was completed, the conversation turned to more personal matters. I could not recognize myself. I had been with Anna for 20 years, from when we were teen-agers, nevertheless, slowly I found the young woman more and more irresistible. The result of the meeting was that nine months later a son was born to the young woman and I was the father. We have kept the secret all these years."

The story that was being unfolded was evidently a great shock to those in the room who knew Don Carini, the lack of comment or interruption underlining the attention each was paying as he spoke. The atmosphere was electric.

Although it was Roberto's wish that Valerie and Peter should hear what had happened, unfortunately at this early stage of their acquaintance with the Italian language neither was able to understand a word of what was being said, particularly because Don Carini spoke with a very strong Sicilian dialect, which can present difficulty even for Italians. Roberto realized that that was the case and promised he would explain everything later. Having interrupted Don Carini to make the promise to the English pair, he went on to suggest that they should return with Claudia to the palace. Peter and Claudia could continue with their wedding ceremony. His marriage to Valerie would have to be delayed for the moment. He had responsibilities to attend to.

"Of course, I agree." Valerie said, then turned to Peter and Claudia with a look that invited their decisions.

Peter and Claudia looked at one another, then, without a word between them, stood and joined Valerie, who was already leaving the room.

Claudia drove and tried to explain a little of the background and history of the relationship between the Grassina and Carini families.

"I was only eight years old at the time, but I still remember clearly the anxiety of our family. Edoardo had met a girl and before he discovered she was Eleanora, the daughter of Carini, it was too late. He was in love with her. They were both only 16 years old and our families did their utmost to discourage them both. It was no use, their love was so strong, even at that tender age, and there was no way they could be kept apart. Two Italian families with such diverse traditions and codes of honor were kept from conflict only by their love for their children. The two families could quite easily have been renamed Montague and Capulet."

Peter interrupted to ask for confirmation that the Carini family were members of the mafia.

"Yes, Don Carini is one of the godfathers. That, of course, was the basic problem. Our family detests the mafia and all it stands for."

Valerie and Peter began to enter a world they were not prepared for, and they were shocked.

Claudia continued, "Unfortunately, the families' efforts to try to keep Edoardo and Eleanora apart had the effect of making them even more determined. Their relationship grew and finally when Edoardo was just 20 years old they were married. There was a positive result to the wedding and that was that the Carini family no longer viewed our family with suspicion and we had no further problems or confrontations with the mafia, as a result of which, and for the sake of

Edoardo and Eleanora, we felt obliged to stop agitating against the mafia, which had been our family policy previously."

The car turned in through the gates of the palace and was immediately surrounded by the women who had remained behind, anxious to know what had happened.

Claudia calmed everyone and led them through to the great sitting room. While the family members were settling down, she turned to Peter, who was beside her, and spoke softly. Valerie was able to see that Peter agreed with whatever it was that Claudia said. She then asked for everyone's attention.

"The first thing I must announce is that both wedding ceremonies are to be postponed." As she spoke she looked across to where Valerie stood. Valerie had anticipated the decision and expressed, facially, her understanding.

Claudia continued to explain to everyone what she had seen and heard at Edoardo's office. This time her clear expression began to make sense to Valerie. Peter, who had joined Valerie in the meantime, turned to her and they both agreed that it had been a dramatic turn-around from the ecstatic happiness of the wedding preparations, in the morning, to this new, horrific situation.

It was two hours later that the series of cars carrying Roberto, Edoardo and the rest of the male members of the family, returned to the palace. As the last car came to a halt in front of the steps to the main entrance, several of the men moved forward and lifted the bodies of Eleanora and her daughter Gina from the back seat of the car, then carried them into the house.

The women, who now had visual evidence of the horror, began to break down, crying and screaming, while the men did their best to comfort them.

Roberto took charge of the situation. Having instructed that the bodies be taken to Eleanora's bedroom, he went to the office to call the carabinieri.

Meanwhile, the family returned to the great hall and were speculating on what might have happened, while Edoardo was unable to face anyone and retired to his room, where he was comforted by Cecilia and Simonetta. Roberto had called the family physician who arrived very quickly and gave Edoardo a strong sedative.

The day was very difficult for Valerie, her mother, and Peter. There was nothing they could do and little they could understand. In the circumstances they decided it best to leave the palace for a few hours and drove into Pisa during the late afternoon, where they wandered aimlessly around the city. Valerie could not help but recall the tenderness of the afternoon she had spent there with Roberto just a few days previously.

It was around midnight when Roberto joined Valerie in the *camera del est.* She was still awake and anxious to know the details of what had transpired.

Roberto told her all he had learned during the course of the day. Apparently each of the three bodies had received a severe blow to the head, although it was not the blow that ended their lives. The cause of death, in each case, was drowning.

Giulio, the bastard son of Carini, had been raised by his mother, Maria, the beautiful young woman Carini met in the hotel. Naturally Carini had taken care of them both. No one knew how Giulio and Eleanora had met and that Eleanora should take her daughter, Gina, with her to the villa of Giulio, was a fact that seemed quite incredulous. The presumption was that they had taken advantage of the fact that Giulio's wife, Tina, had had to travel to Bologna earlier that morning, where she had an appointment with her lawyer. As it happened shortly before arriving in Bologna she realized she had left some important documents at home and decided it necessary to return to the villa.

Giulio had told Tina he had business in the city and would be away for the day, consequently when she arrived home she assumed there would be no one in the house.

The villa was quiet as Tina went through to the small den where she knew the papers to be. She located the file and was about to leave to return to Bologna when she heard noises that appeared to come from the area of the pool. She feared there were intruders; so, before making her way as quietly as she could to the pool area, she armed herself with the large wooden club Giulio always kept under the bed for security.

She left the villa through a side door that led to the garden and as she approached the pool area she began to realize that the noises she was hearing were those of people happily enjoying themselves in the pool. Then her flesh began to tingle and her pulse began to race as she realized that one of the voices she was hearing was that of her husband, Giulio.

For a few minutes she remained secreted in some bushes near the pool and listened and watched as Giulio laughed and played in the water with a young woman and a girl. They caressed gently and gave the impression of being very much in love.

Soon Tina could stand it no more. In a fit of rage and jealousy she stepped forward and made her presence known to her treacherous husband and his female companions.

Giulio, Eleanora, and Gina moved toward the edge of the pool, where Tina stood trembling and screaming. They were anxious to calm her. Tina was not to be calmed and as they reached the edge of the pool she raised the wooden club above her head and with all her force struck Giulio on the head, then immediately raised it once more and proceeded to meter the same punishment to Eleanora. Both slumped back, their lungs began to fill with water and slowly their bodies sank, a series of bubbles marking their watery graves. Gina in horror and desperation attempted to reach the other side of the pool. She had no chance and shortly left her own trail of bubbles rising to the surface.

Don Carini assumed full responsibility for what had happened, saying that had he not deceived his wife or, having done so had had the courage to declare the fact and make the siblings known to one another, the terrible event would not have occurred.

When he left the office building, Carini told Roberto and the rest of the family members, that he intended to take his own life following the funeral of his son. He had prosecuted, found himself guilty and pronounced the death sentence. In such circumstances there was no question of dissuading him from his decision.

The carabinieri had issued a warrant for the arrest of Tina, although there was little possibility she would be found because Carini had given orders that she should be protected by the family. She was not to blame, and was probably already in Sicily.

Following Roberto's call to the carabinieri the bodies of Eleanora and Gina were taken to join that of Giulio at the morgue, where post-mortems would be carried out to confirm the causes of death.

The major puzzle was how had Eleanora and Giulio met and when. Could they have been lovers?

The atmosphere at *Il Palazzo* changed dramatically in just a few hours, from joy to somber. The Baron's death had plunged the whole family into a state of profound sadness. He had been a very popular and respected head of the family. The circumstances surrounding his death, that had been responsible for bringing Roberto and Valerie together, had, in some way, made it possible for the family to go on and Roberto's decision to marry Valerie so quickly had the effect of breathing new life into the melancholy situation.

Roberto and Valerie knew almost from the moment they first met, even in circumstances that seemed completely non-conducive to such an accord, that they were born to be with one another. Roberto's suggestion that they should marry, two days after the funeral of the Baron, was a diplomatic coup, as far as the family situation was concerned. He assumed leadership of the family by heredity and took advantage of their unique gathering. However, instead of a double wedding there was now to be a double funeral. It was impossible to conjecture as to when the Quartet would be in a position to consider their own futures or happiness. The current situation was far too serious and complex.

Valerie insisted that Roberto remain with her, once again her duty being to comfort him. She held him in her arms throughout the night and neither slept.

Italian tradition is that the bereaved should not be alone at times of loss. The entire family had paid their respects to Edoardo and as the news spread flowers and messages began to arrive from the many who respected the Grassina family. In Edoardo's room the two bodies had been dressed and laid side by side on the bed, Eleanora's left hand resting on Gina's right. In their other hands each held rosaries. The recorded sounds of the Verdi requiem mass muted the continued weeping of the women who came and went. Not for one moment was Edoardo left alone, everyone sharing the grief of the husband and father.

The next morning, at a very early hour, an unexpected caller arrived at the palace, a courier from the British Embassy in Bucharest. He was shown to one of the reception rooms to await the arrival of Roberto, who was informed. Roberto excused himself with Valerie, then quickly went down to meet the courier. It was only a very few minutes before Valerie, Peter, and Claudia were summoned to the reception room also.

The courier had with him a letter from the ambassador. Roberto read the contents to the other members of the Quartet.

My dear friends,

I find myself in a very distressing situation. A situation I can only relate to you and hope that you may see your way clear to try to assist me.

By my previous marriage I had a son, John, from whom I have not heard for several months. A week ago I had a call from his mother who was very alarmed. It would seem that John, who is an artist, took his wife, Kate, and their two-month-old baby daughter, Sarah, to Florence, with the intention of visiting the Uffizi gallery.

John promised he would telephone his mother as soon as they arrived at the hotel. His mother has a very nervous disposition and would not rest until she knew they had arrived safely.

The flight was due to land in Florence during the afternoon. At 11 p.m. my ex-wife called the hotel, having heard nothing. They had not checked in. She then called the airline who confirmed that the flight had arrived on time and that the three passengers had been on board. It was then she decided to call me.

I had my security staff begin inquiries immediately. As of today they have exhausted all avenues of inquiry, including contacts with the police in Florence, and have no leads whatever. I enclose photographs together with all the information I could assemble.

I place myself at your disposition. Roberto, if you feel unable to help me, perhaps you could suggest someone of your acquaintance, and from your experience, whom you consider could be counted on to act swiftly and efficiently to try and locate our family.

Yours,

Ralph Carter-Barnes,
Ambassador,
British Embassy,
Bucharest,
Rumania.

Roberto slowly lowered his hand holding the letter and with a desperate tone said, "Well, my friends, we are in a dilemma. However, I am confident that, like me, you wish to investigate the loss of the ambassador's family. It is something we *must* do. I know this city well and have many contacts. There is no time to lose." As he spoke Roberto took a sheet of paper from a beautiful inlaid desk and replied to the ambassador's letter.

Your Excellency,

My friends and I will commence our inquiries immediately and will report back to you anything and everything we discover.

You may be assured of our support and sorrow during your present situation. We have recently sustained a severe blow to our own family and can sympathize.

Further details shortly.

Your friends,

The note was signed by all four and handed to the courier who left immediately for Florence airport, where the ambassador's aircraft was waiting to return him to Bucharest.

Roberto felt that Carini, with his underworld contacts, might be able to assist in locating the lost family. He took Valerie with him, following her insistance that she was not happy for him to go alone. They drove across the city and up into the hills on the opposite side of the Arno river, arriving at a beautiful, gothic style, country mansion.

Valerie wished to be with Roberto, nevertheless as they drove through the gates and on up to the house she felt the beat of her heart increase and her hands begin to perspire. She had an instinctive fear of Carini.

They were shown through to the library where Carini sat in his dressing gown, the shadow of the man they had seen the previous day.

Roberto came straight to the point. He explained the problem and suggested that this was an opportunity for Carini to perform one positive act before he took his life.

Yet again Valerie was unable to understand Carini's reply and was obliged to wait for Roberto's explanation as they returned to the palace.

Carini had heard of an organization, not associated with the mafia, that abducted whole tourist families who were travelling with very young children. The babies were sold for adoption, while the parents were forced into illegal acts on the promise that eventually they would be reunited.

Previously Carini had no interest in the organization but assured Roberto he would make inquiries.

If the family of the ambassador had indeed been abducted by such a ruthless organization it was now even more urgent to find them.

Roberto and Valerie had just entered *Il Palazzo*, when the crunch of gravel under tires heralded the arrival of the carabinieri. The Maresciallo (Chief Inspector) had been a long-time friend of Roberto and when he became aware of some vital information relating to the deaths of Eleanora and Gina, he wasted no time in bringing it to the attention of his friend.

"Good day, Roberto, Valerie. Forgive my disturbing you once more but I know you would wish to have the latest information I have received."

"I thank you, my friend. Tell me what you have learned," Roberto replied, his eyes firmly fixed on what was obviously a diary the Maresciallo held in his hand.

"This is the diary of Giulio Carini. It was delivered to my office yesterday evening by Don Carini. I have been studying it practically all night. My conclusion is that Giulio and Eleanora met by chance just five days ago. I'm sure you will appreciate that I must retain the diary as evidence. I therefore decided to leave you a print-out of the entries relative to his meeting with Eleanora. You are the best one to convey the details to Edoardo. I am confident that you will undertake that difficult task much better than I could hope to do."

Roberto took the envelope from the Maresciallo, thanking him for his kindness and went on to inform him of what had happened earlier that morning, in relation to the ambassador.

The Maresciallo assured Roberto he would do anything he could to help track down the family of the ambassador. He was already aware of the matter and his detectives were doing the best they could, but so far had unearthed nothing.

Roberto offered his thanks and the Maresciallo left.

While Valerie and Roberto sat drinking coffee, he explained to her he had decided that because there were now two complex matters to follow it would be advisable to begin entering the information onto computer discs, a job ideally suited to Peter.

During the time that Valerie and Roberto were visiting Carini, Peter and Claudia had gone to the office in the city to begin to prepare and duplicate details of the Ambassador's family. A telephone call confirmed they were still working there and Roberto and Valerie hurried to catch them before they left.

By the time they arrived, Peter and Claudia had finished preparing the data and were anxious to begin their inquiries.

Peter took a copy of the police extracts from Giulio's diary and promised to begin creating files on the two subjects later, once they had begun the initial step of their investigation, which they had decided was to visit the bars nearest to where airline passengers alight on their arrival in the city center.

Having received such appalling news in the same offices only one day before and being obliged to pass the same conference room where they had seen the bodies on the oak table, the adrenalin that had been pumping in the veins of the Quartet, with their new tasks, was temporarily subdued, until the two couples left the building and set off to undertake their individual assignments.

Three

The priority for Roberto and Valerie was to return to *Il Palazzo* and speak to Edoardo. However painful the diary entries would be for him, he would certainly wish to know the contents. Now that both Roberto and Valerie knew the details, they felt in some way it might help Edoardo to discover what had been the fundamental cause of the death of Eleanora and Gina.

Edoardo was a good Catholic and lover of nature, consequently, while Roberto and Valerie were involved with their meetings he had, earlier that morning, gone to the family chapel to pray and was now walking in the grounds. Aunt Cecilia suggested where Roberto and Valerie might find him and they began to walk out of the palace. They hadn't far to go.

The stooped figure slowly shuffling across the lawn toward the house, they hardly recognized as Edoardo. He moved like a lost soul, unshaven, his hair dishevelled and still wearing a dressing gown over his pyjamas. Roberto and Valerie felt a great sense of pity for him and found difficulty in holding back the tears. Just twenty-four hours before

Edoardo had been elegantly dressed and upright, the legs that had carried him up some of the highest mountains in the world moving with a powerful gait, debonair and handsome with his unequalled ability to organize. It seemed impossible that such a dramatic transformation could take place in just one day.

The three moved to a stone seat under an oak tree, where Roberto and Edoardo had played as boys. There Roberto told him of the discovery of the diary and handed him the pages. Edoardo declined to accept them.

"Please read it to me," he mumbled.

Roberto glanced at Valerie and expressed by his look his apprehension at the daunting task that now faced him. To prepare him Valerie took Edoardo's hand and kissed him gently on the cheek.

Roberto began reading:

"Monday, October 4th, 1993. I do not know why I am recording such events. I am a happily married man who had no intention of cheating on his wife. The young woman I met this morning was truly beautiful but that was not the reason for my attraction to her. The reason is a mystery to me. I felt I knew her and yet I knew I did not.

"Just an innocent moment in front of a coffee bar, sitting at a table beneath the trees on an early autumn morning. The bustle of the traffic on the crowded streets, the happiness of the people because the air they breathed not only gave life but carried joy to their souls. Then beside me an angel slipped on the cobblestones and made a gentle cry as she twisted her ankle. I helped her to the chair beside me, then called the waiter to bring a glass of water and a coffee for her.

"I felt protective toward her, as a brother would feel for a sister."

Roberto paused from his reading for a moment and glanced at Edoardo. How strange that Giulio should make such a note in his diary. He recommenced his reading.

"Her eyes met mine and my heart quivered. We did not speak but I sensed she also felt something for me.

"I lifted her ankle onto my lap and very gently moved the joint, to ensure that nothing was broken. I then massaged her ankle gently and she took two aspirins the waiter had thoughtfully brought with the water.

"Time seemed suspended and the song of the birds, as if directed by an orchestral conductor, slowly augmented in volume, replacing the noise of the traffic.

"I felt as though we had come together after many years, we had so many things to speak of and yet we said nothing.

"Soon we were walking, hand in hand, in the light, sweet rain that had begun to fall. Time passed slowly yet quickly and then I became aware that we were on a country lane outside the city. Her fall had been less serious than had at first appeared and she walked with only a very slight limp.

"I stopped her and stepped two paces forward. There I turned and gazed at her once more. The rain had drenched her thin summer dress, which had become almost transparent. Beneath she wore only the slightest pair of panties and I felt a strong, overwhelming desire for her. I believe that her eyes were also devouring me. I removed my long summer raincoat and covered her with it, feeling no shame as I kissed her softly on the lips.

"The kiss was beautiful and new so why did I have the feeling I had known her all my life. I had never seen her before. Who was she?

"Our bodies joined together in a firm embrace. We did not fulfill the act of lovemaking but arrived at a point so near to that blissful state as to almost make a mockery of the definition.

"Before parting we promised to meet again, the day after tomorrow, just for an hour. It would be all the time she could spare. Her family expected her for a very important function.

"What have I done? I did not mention that I am married and have a good and faithful wife. On recollection I realize we hardly spoke at all. The next time we meet, two days, a lifetime, I must be patient, I will tell her everything. Something is very strange about her, about our meeting, and together with the pounding in my heart, I also have a sensation of fear."

"How cruel, fate," Edoardo muttered, "a brother and sister meet and misinterpret the natural, instinctive feelings they have for one another, because of the blood relationship, believing it to be love. That they should die!"

"Come back to the house now," Valerie encouraged, "the severity of the situation has drained all your strength and you ----"

"They are gone," Edoardo interrupted. "Had it been a car accident or some illness I could perhaps have come to terms with it in time but I see no possibility of understanding why two wonderful, young people should be trapped in a fate from which there was no chance of escape." As Edoardo spoke Roberto and Valerie helped him to his feet and the three went into the house.

Edoardo took a couple of the pills left for him by the family physician, and lay on a chaise longue in the anteroom of the dining room. Roberto and Valerie remained with him while he drifted off to sleep, then went and found Cecilia who happily agreed to sit with Edoardo.

"I would dearly like to stay with my cousin and help him through this terrible period but we must act quickly to try to locate the ambassador's family. Come on, Valerie, I have an idea."

Roberto and Valerie were about to leave the palace when they were called back for a telephone call from Claudia. They went back inside and Roberto picked up the telephone.

"What have you discovered?" Roberto anticipated.

In a few seconds he replaced the receiver.

"Come on, we must go back to the city, Claudia and Peter have a lead already."

Valerie wondered whether Roberto was ever stopped for speeding.

"No, I normally remain near enough to the limit, but since we met it seems that every time we are in a car we are also in a great hurry."

Claudia and Peter were waiting on the forecourt of a small restaurant and were almost jumping up and down with excitement when the car drew up alongside them.

Soon the four, led by Peter, were inside the restaurant, walking briskly between the tables, most of which had been set for the evening guests.

In a dimly lit corner, one table was occupied by an old man. Peter spoke quietly to him for a moment, then in perfect German, introduced his friends to Herr Kurt Ansorg.

Apparently the carabinieri could not be bothered with him because he spoke no Italian, and unwittingly overlooked the very one who could assist them. Yet again Peter's command of that language had proven very convenient.

Ansorg was sitting with his feet on a second chair and his knees raised, supporting a board on which he had a pad of sketching paper. Peter explained that Ansorg was virtually a permanent resident at the restaurant and spent his day making caricatures of the diners, some of whom paid him for his work and took home yet another memory of their visit to Florence.

He had been there on the day of arrival of the ambassador's family. They could not afford to buy his sketches, consequently when Peter showed Ansorg the photographs, it was necessary only to look through the stack of drawings that had accumulated and there they were. What was so exciting to Peter and Claudia was that, not only were John, Katy and baby Sarah depicted in the sketch, but there was a fourth figure also. To the best of his memory Ansorg thought the four had arrived and left together.

Roberto handed the old man a 100,000 lira note (approximately $60), and took possession of the sketch.

The Quartet could not believe their luck. They had been prepared for an intensive investigation and possibly no clues for a very long time. Peter and Claudia had pre-selected five locations to begin with. The restaurant had been the first on their list and, as it transpired, the relevant one.

Armed with new hope and optimism the four set off together, their destination this time being the Questura (police headquarters). There they would show the drawing to the Maresciallo in the hope that the fourth figure could be identified from police records.

There was considerable enthusiasm at the Questura when the drawing was produced and a loud 'Bravo' from the Maresciallo, though there followed a slight disappointment. The figure in the drawing was not immediately recognizable, not that that was final. The section of the sketch depicting the unknown figure was enlarged and enhanced by a police artist and copies made and circulated.

Roberto's idea, before they were called to Florence, had to be shelved once more. It would be necessary to make a further call on Carini. If he was prepared to help he could circulate the description amongst his underworld associates. It was worth a try.

Claudia and Peter, after their early success, decided to continue checking bars and restaurants in the hope that someone else may have also seen the family, while Roberto and Valerie left for the Carini villa once more.

On the journey Valerie asked when the funerals of Eleanora and Gina might take place.

"The funerals can't be arranged until the post-mortems have been completed and the bodies released by the court," Roberto explained. "I am sure that Edoardo will wish to deal with the arrangements himself, despite his deep sorrow. In the meantime we must keep lines of communication open to the palace. The information could arrive at any moment. The funeral service will obviously take priority."

Just six hours had elapsed since Roberto and Valerie last called at Carini's residence and the bodyguards were surprised to see them back again so soon. Roberto asked to see Carini and they were shown through to a downstairs room.

The room they entered was dimly lit and both became apprehensive until the lights were switched on. At the far end of the room was a dais on which stood a coffin with the lid open. Roberto and Valerie presumed it to be the coffin of Giulio.

"You asked to see Don Carini. I am afraid you may only see him, it will not be possible to speak to him. Please." They were urged to move toward the coffin. As they drew closer and the contents came into view they were both shocked to see that it was Carini himself whose cold body lay in the casket, and not Giulio.

"This is just terrible," Roberto exclaimed. "What on earth happened? I suppose he committed suicide, but he said he would wait until after the funeral of Giulio."

"He intended to wait," the guard replied, "unfortunately Edoardo changed his mind for him. Now we have two corpses and your family has one more, because having shot Don Carini through the heart with a single bullet, Edoardo then turned the pistol on himself and pulled the trigger once more."

Roberto quickly availed himself of a chair before his legs gave way. The series of shocks appeared never-ending. He had loved Edoardo almost as much as his father. They had been more like brothers than cousins.

Valerie had a very morbid sensation at the sight of yet another corpse but she suppressed her feelings and spoke firmly to Roberto at a time when she would have preferred to comfort him. She felt he needed her to be strong on this occasion.

"Roberto, the family needs you more than ever now. It is your burden to lift them above all the disasters. I think we need to go to the Questura once more."

"You are right, my dear," Roberto replied, his voice audibly gaining strength as his mind brought his bodily functions back to full potency. "We will return immediately to the Questura."

The news of the deaths of Carini and Edoardo had just been received at the Questura when Roberto and Valerie arrived.

"Good God, Roberto, there is no justification for such a terrible series of misfortunes and we need to discuss your latest loss but first I want to give you some good news. Thirty minutes after you left we had a reply from Interpol regarding the figure in the sketch. He has been identified as Henry Le Pen, an international criminal figure, born in

Belgium in 1947. His contribution to society includes his being wanted in the Philippines for a huge swindle involving Australian sheep exports."

The Maresciallo intelligently kept speaking, giving Roberto no time to think about the loss of his cousin. "Wanted also in Peru, and Bolivia, under suspicion of kidnapping babies. Evidence has also linked him to an organization involved in the trading of body parts for transplants. A very unpleasant character indeed. His whereabouts are unknown but we already have many good photographs of him and a great deal of information."

Roberto fixed his mind on this new important information. He couldn't help his cousin anymore but it was urgent to find the family of the ambassador.

"Then it would appear that what Carini told us has some possible foundation. An adoption racket. I haven't had the opportunity to tell you but this morning we went to see Carini. He suggested such an organization and went on to say that probably the wife would be forced into prostitution and some blackmail hold employed in the case of the husband, suggesting that if they carried out the tasks given them they would ultimately be reunited. We need to find these poor devils and fast."

"Don't worry, old friend. We have circulated full descriptions and I am confident we will hear something very soon. I am concerned about the baby. There is a good possibility she has been taken out of the country already, the most likely destination being the U.S.A. There are many rich, desperate people there who will ask no questions if the transaction is simple."

"I think it is time to return to the palace," Valerie interjected. "The other members of the family should be informed."

"You are right," Roberto replied. "Let's go."

Valerie began to realize what tremendous will-power Roberto possessed. Even after such appalling events he was able to force himself to put the family first.

On their arrival at the palace Roberto instructed the butler to find Cecilia and Simonetta and bring them to the anteroom where they had last seen Edoardo alive.

They had to wait only a few minutes.

"Roberto, Valerie, I am so glad you have returned, Edoardo insisted on going alone, but I am worried. He has been gone three hours now and I really don't know where he is."

"Cecilia, Simonetta," Roberto took their hands, "I'm sorry but I have some more bad news."

"Oh no, not Edoardo too."

"Yes, I am afraid so. He obviously held Carini totally responsible for the deaths of Eleanora and Gina. Having disposed of Carini he then took his own life. The whole matter is so sad. You know I still remember the day I opened my eyes and was able to see for the first time, everything was so perfect, we were a close and happy family, the future seemed to hold so many good prospects. Then there was Valerie," he glanced at her. "I don't know how I could have coped with all the terrible things that have happened without her."

Cecilia and Simonetta were both speechless and slowly tears began to run down their sweet old faces. Valerie and Roberto did the best they could to comfort them.

"Unfortunately, Valerie, Claudia, Peter and I must be away a great deal at the moment until we are able to find the family of the ambassador. I must ask you two good kind ladies to convey the latest dreadful news to the rest of the family."

Cecilia and Simonetta had lived through four generations and witnessed the deaths of many members of the family, though nothing so catastrophic as the losses of the family so loved by every member of the Grassina's. They also had a very high regard for Roberto and Claudia and knew that what they were undertaking was a very just cause.

"Don't worry, we will take care of everything, you concentrate on finding that poor family."

For a moment Roberto, Valerie and the aunts just sat in silence, then the chimes of midnight on the grandfather clock made them aware that it had been thirty-six hours since they last had any sleep. Valerie commented that in films and on television investigators don't seem to need sleep. They on the other hand had to be prepared for the day ahead.

"Come, sister, we must call the family together and inform them of what has happened," Simonetta asserted as she stood and took Cecilia's hand. Roberto and Valerie both kissed the two old ladies on their cheeks, then left.

It was early morning when Roberto glanced at Valerie, where she lay beside him. Then he very gently stroked her forehead with the backs of his fingers.

"They were so beautiful," Valerie whispered.

"Who were?" Roberto queried.

"The birds, many small, coloured birds."

"You were dreaming of birds?"

"Yes, and I heard them singing, such delicate, sweet melodies."

Roberto continued to caress her forehead and changed the subject.

"Do you remember when we were about to leave yesterday, I said I had an idea?"

"Yes, tell me."

"Well, six months ago I dragged a young woman from the Arno river, she had tried to commit suicide. At first she was not happy to have been saved but we talked for a long time and slowly she began to be glad that she had failed in her suicide attempt. She had reluctantly become involved with a call girl agency, trying to get quick money for her father whose business had serious financial problems. I found her a place in our offices and loaned her father the money to clear his debts. He has since rebuilt his business and paid back the loan. The girl has also done very well in the office. It may be that she can give us some ideas to help us find the daughter of the ambassador."

"Let's go, I can be ready in half an hour."

Roberto kissed Valerie gently and they began to prepare themselves for another day.

Four

Roberto and Valerie had spent the night together in the *camera del est*. The beauty Valerie experienced on the first occasion she slept there was repeated, with a stunning sunrise. It would have been impossible to overlook such an event, even so, under the circumstances, they both awoke with low spirits and were unable to derive the full benefit of the golden light that filled the room.

Valerie was very saddened by the series of deaths that had occurred during the previous ten days. She hardly knew the Baron, Eleanora, Gina, or Edoardo but by her love for Roberto she had instantly accepted all his family as if they were her own. They had likewise responded. Even so the loss was obviously much greater for Roberto and she felt she must give him all the love and support she could summon.

They had been robbed of their glorious wedding night and even though they were, to all intents and purposes, living together as husband and wife, somehow it was not the same. They could not emulate the two occasions they had made full, passionate love and which had been so extraordinary for Valerie. She was anxiously anticipating the next occasion. That could not happen until time had completed its healing process and the planned wedding taken place. Both realized that.

Throughout the night just past, they had both slept naked, their bodies had touched, they had kissed and caressed but neither had the desire to go beyond the gentleness of their embraces.

Roberto went to his office to make telephone calls and write letters, leaving Valerie with her thoughts.

While she prepared herself she recalled her dream of the little coloured birds and how Roberto had been so gentle with her. She could do much to help alleviate his pain by giving him visual pleasure. He made no secret of how much he admired her beauty. She would pay particular attention to her appearance which, when added to her encouragement in the search for the family of the ambassador, would utilize a major percentage of his thoughts, thereby taking his mind from the family tragedies. There was one other effort she must make. She must lift herself out of her own depression and sadness and by doing so fulfill her duty completely.

She was ready in half an hour, as promised, and as she entered the office Roberto looked up from his letter writing.

"You look magnificent, darling Valerie," Roberto complimented as he drank in her beauty from head to toe. The first stage had been successful.

"Thank you, Roberto. I was thinking about the suggestion you made last night, concerning the girl from your office. It seems very well worth pursuing. Do you intend to go there this morning?" Valerie responded with a delicate smile on her lips.

"I have already sent a car to bring the girl here and, oh, Peter and Claudia are waiting for us in the dining room.

Shall we join them? That will give us the opportunity to analyze what we have so far."

"Fine. I am raring to go."

"Just one thing first." Roberto could resist no longer. He moved closer to her, placed his arm around her waist and met her lips with his in a kiss that seemed to melt their lips together. They seemed reluctant to draw apart, but it was necessary to suppress any desire and he frivolously remarked, as their lips finally separated, that her lipstick tasted very good.

"That was wonderful and a new promise for the future, I am sure," Valerie smiled as she took both his hands in hers. "Time will cure all the sadness and we will be together. The family will reassert itself and I am also confident we will find the ambassador's family. Roberto, I love you very much."

"And I you too."

The anteroom to the dining room began to take on the appearance of an operations center. Roberto had arranged to have a computer system installed for Peter to work on and there were enlarged photographs of the ambassador's family together with the enhanced drawing of the man featured in the Ansorg sketch, all pinned to boards resting on easels.

The Quartet greeted one another, then Peter handed a file to each of them.

During the night a fax had arrived and was included with the material in the file. Roberto now saw it for the first time. It had come from the Maresciallo at the Questura and confirmed that the man in the drawing had reportedly arrived in Florida the day before yesterday. He was accompanied by a woman and baby. From the immigration records it was doubtful that the woman was the mother of the child, as she was Puerto Rican, whereas the child was white. There was no information as to where they had gone after their arrival in Orlando.

The four discussed at length the evidence they had accumulated and it was decided that Claudia and Peter would leave for Florida on the first available flight. It was essential to find baby Sarah as soon as possible, not that they believed her to be in danger but the longer the time span the hazier the original details would become, and by now the child had certainly been given a new identity.

Roberto called his secretary and instructed her to arrange the flight for Peter and Claudia. As he replaced the receiver the girl from the office arrived. She appeared very nervous, perhaps fearing some trouble. When Roberto realized that that was the case he instantly put her mind at rest and went on to explain the problem.

She was anxious to help her benefactor and divulged everything she could remember concerning the call girl agency and the Madame for whom she had been working, before her attempted suicide. Roberto assured her he would not reveal his source of information. The girl made a suggestion that would give them easy access to the organization. She remarked how attractive both Valerie and Claudia were and said she was confident the agency would not hesitate to offer both of them work, by which method, and in time, they would meet all the other girls, who were called to a meeting once a month. She recalled that the meetings always occurred on the 10th, although the location was different each time and a secret until the evening before. Today being the 7th there was little time to lose.

Roberto thanked the girl and she was taken back to the office in the city.

Valerie's look evidently suggested she was prepared to try to make contact.

"No, it's too risky," Roberto snapped.

"It's our only chance at the moment. We have no idea where to begin to look for the father. If we can find the mother, maybe we could trace back through the contacts of the Madame and that way locate the father also."

"We will do it together," Claudia confirmed. "Peter and I must delay our trip to the U.S.A. for a few days. There is no question of your being on your own."

Roberto and Peter were both uneasy with the idea, until Peter suggested he could call the agency as a potential client, saying he wanted two girls, girls who had never worked before and would be prepared to pay extra. By that method they would hope to obviate the possibility of the girls' being called upon to meet clients.

"Let's begin by making contact with the Madame," Roberto suggested. "I am known in the city but I could say I am looking for company in my hour of sadness."

"That's a reasonable idea," Peter retorted

Roberto called the number given him by the girl. "My name is Roberto Grassina, maybe you know who I am." Roberto nodded indicating that the person he was calling apparently did know of him. "I need to be sure of the utmost discretion ..... I would like to meet one of your girls ..... For this occasion I would prefer that she were not Italian ..... English, yes, that would be fine, is tonight possible? ..... Where must I go .... OK, I will be there at 8."

After replacing the receiver Roberto suggested perhaps the English girl he was to meet could be Kate, but that was too much to hope for.

Peter thought it might be useful to have some system of communication and Claudia agreed to take him to an electronics store in the city. There he would find whatever was necessary.

In the meantime Roberto called his secretary once more telling her to cancel the flight booking for Peter and Claudia. If his evening appointment proved unsuccessful Claudia and Valerie would try to make contact with the Madame.

"Don't let's waste time," Claudia suggested. "We can make contact today. Time is of the essence."

"Very well," Roberto replied reluctantly, "but you had better wait until this evening and Claudia will need to disguise herself in some way. She could be recognized."

"No problem, with makeup anything is possible. I can also wear clear glasses and gaudy clothes. That way even you wouldn't know me."

The four spent the rest of the day, until 4 p.m., on the telephone to adoption agencies in Florida. They discovered five that seemed to think they could find a suitable baby without too much formality.

Now it was the turn of Claudia, who trembled as the number of the Madame rang and did not settle down even after replacing the receiver. She was anxious to assist in any way possible but she and Valerie were about to place themselves in a very precarious situation.

The Madame invited Claudia and Valerie for an appointment at midnight. They would be collected from a bar by the Ponte Vecchio on the bank of the Arno river. From there they would be taken to an unspecified destination to be evaluated. If they were found to be suitable, there was a possibility they could begin meeting clients within a couple of days.

Roberto decided it would not be wise to tell the Maresciallo of their plans. They would have to just hope that if they got into any difficulty he would mobilize his men very quickly to help.

At 8 p.m. Roberto drove to the prescribed meeting place. Soon a very attractive, tall, slim girl arrived who in no way resembled Kate.

"Let's first drive around for a while," Roberto suggested. "I prefer to take my time. How long can you stay?"

"You are my last appointment for today, I can stay the night if you like but it will cost you 500,000 lire." ($300).

The car pulled away and Roberto flicked the switch under the dash, activating the small transmitter Peter had installed during the afternoon.

Back at *Il Palazzo*, Peter, Claudia, and Valerie heard clearly what was being said in the car and grinned at one another when they heard Roberto tell the girl it was not necessary for her to touch him for the time being. He had problems and just wanted to talk.

Roberto manipulated the conversation as much as he could, just appearing genuinely curious, but learned very little. Probably the girls would never know when the agency might send someone to check that they were keeping their mouths shut and were very careful.

"Listen, you are a very attractive young lady and I don't want to offend you. You have been very kind to listen to me all evening but I think I would like to go home now."

"That's all right, dear, the price is the same. It's my time you are paying for."

"Just as a curiosity are there many non-Italian girls working for your agency? I see Italian girls all day long and when I am more myself I would like to see you again and maybe some of the other girls too."

"I know of four Germans, if you like them big, and one other English girl. She joined recently, but she is very moody."

"In that case I will definitely ask for you. Where can I drop you?"

"I live just a few streets from here. Just let me out. I'll walk, it'll do me good."

"OK, good bye, it has been a pleasure meeting you."

"Thank you, dear, I wish there were more like you, good bye."

There was a short pause, then the voice of Roberto once more,

"I hope you got all that."

By now Peter was the only one monitoring the signal, Valerie and Claudia had left to prepare themselves for their meeting.

Roberto arrived back at *Il Palazzo* just after 11:30 p.m., by which time the girls had already left.

Peter had concealed a transmitter in a necklace Valerie was wearing, which impressed Roberto very much and he complimented Peter on his knowledge, to which Peter responded he had specialized in that type of work for the past ten years.

"We are just arriving at Ponte Vecchio," said the clear but shaky voice of Valerie over the loudspeaker. "This will be the last time I can say anything. From now on you will have to pick up what you can from our conversation."

"I don't like it," Roberto said, thumping the table with his fist.

Peter calmed him by saying he had also installed a receiver in the BMW and if things began to get out of hand they would be able to track the girls down.

The bug picked up the sound of the car door opening. Then a man's voice.

"Don't tell us your names. We don't want to know and you will not know the names of anyone you meet either. Come with us."

Sounds indicated Valerie and Claudia transferring to another car. The journey took approximately fifteen minutes, during which time not a word was spoken, following the statement of one of the men who said they were only taking the girls to a meeting place and knew nothing else and there was to be no talking.

They arrived at a deserted building on the outskirts of the city and were shown into a room that was immediately lit up with very powerful lights. Valerie and Claudia were instructed to move to the middle of the room, remove their jackets and raise their skirts. There was silence for a moment, then a woman's voice,

"From now on you will be working for me. You will know me as Angelina, that of course is not my real name. The day after tomorrow there will be our once-a-month meeting. There you will be given a medical checkup and details of how we operate. You on the left will be called Donna and the other Carla. For today that's everything. You will now be taken back to Ponte Vecchio."

Both Peter and Roberto breathed a sigh of relief. Hopefully, because of the short time before the meeting on the 10th, they would not be called upon to meet clients, especially as they were to have a medical checkup first.

Half an hour later the two couples were hugging each other, pleased with the result so far. Everyone was tired and decided it was time for bed.

Both Claudia and Valerie were looking magnificent in their figure-hugging suits, Claudia in midnight blue which complemented her cascading, jet black hair, while Valerie wore white, which also contrasted very well with her auburn hair. They had both emphasized their makeup and accessories in an attempt to look the part and the final result had the effect of inspiring both Roberto and Peter.

The day had been a strain on everyone's nerves, gentle love-making for both couples would now have the effect of seductive sedation.

The following morning the four had their minds concentrated on the task of finding the family, a task that they were subconsciously utilizing to shield them from the sorrows closer to home. However, the arrival of the Maresciallo, at an early hour, compelled them to concentrate once more on the family.

By now the Maresciallo had come to accept that anything he had to say to Roberto would include the other three and he was content to wait until all four were present.

He decided it would be best to give the reports in a cold and formal manner:

"The coroner's reports have been completed in the cases of Eleanora and Gina. In each case death was due to asphyxia as a result of the intake of water to the lungs following the blows to the heads, which caused fracturing in each case. Both were unconscious before they drowned. It has also been concluded that Edoardo died as the result of a single gunshot to the head and death is presumed to have been instantaneous. Foul play is not suspected in Edoardo's death, and it is now in order to arrange the funerals for all three. We are endeavoring to locate Tina, who as you know is believed to be responsible for the blows received by Giulio, Eleanora and Gina."

"I want to thank you," Roberto said, "for arranging to deal with everything so quickly. You know how important it is for us to be able to put our loved ones to rest. I will notify the family and begin to make the arrangements."

The Maresciallo understood that this was not the time to speak of any other matters, confirmed his condolences and excused himself.

Roberto called a meeting of all the family members and it was agreed that the funerals would take place on the 10th. The selection of the date prompted the Quartet to recall the other event that would occur that day. The timing was very delicate but there was no question of delaying the funerals.

Claudia took Peter to help her select the floral arrangements while Roberto remained at *Il Palazzo* making telephone calls.

He first called the undertaker, who had agreed to arrange the triple funeral. The remains would be laid to rest in the family chapel at *Il Palazzo*.

He then called the Bishop who was to have conducted the double wedding. He was inflexible and frustrated Roberto by his refusal to consecrate the remains of Edoardo. Roberto was equally adamant that the casket would lie in the chapel, alongside those of his wife and daughter. The Bishop appreciated that in similar circumstances he would have been just as emphatic had he lost three of his nearest and dearest relatives within such a short span of time and agreed that the service would be worded in such a way as to overcome the difficulties arising from the fact that Edoardo had taken his own life.

After replacing the receiver Roberto became very angry and was calmed only by the other three who pointed out that the Bishop had really exceeded his possibilities considerably, placing himself in a position of conflict with the church, something that would have repercussions for him for a long time.

The terrible losses did in fact have the effect of strengthening the family, and Valerie and Peter were amazed at the deep feeling demonstrated between the relatives.

The final arrangements were that the funeral service would be held at 11 a.m. They could only hope that the meeting with the Madame would be much later in the day.

Five

During the morning the answering service had received a call for Claudia. She was to call the Madame. They hadn't expected a call so soon and Claudia's heart began to beat fast when she realized what she must do. There was of course no question of Claudia keeping an appointment, but they hadn't yet considered how they would deal with such an eventuality. The four gathered round as Claudia made the call.

An important client of the agency had expressed a desire for a girl with typical Sicilian characteristics; long black hair, dark eyes and Mediterranean complexion. Claudia met the criteria and was instructed she must be punctual for a 10 p.m. appointment at the Duomo hotel that evening. Following the appointment she would receive information concerning the following day's meeting. She asked what time the meeting would be and was told never to ask questions again, just to obey instructions. That way there would be no problems.

In a desperate attempt to change the arrangement, Peter waited thirty minutes, then telephoned the Madame, explaining he was in town for one night and wished to have two girls for the evening. He was prepared to pay double if the girls were good enough.

There was a delay, then the message came back that it would be possible but he should call again one hour later.

The tension mounted as they waited but no call came through for Claudia. They had been hoping that the arrangements already made would be changed and Claudia and Valerie would be assigned to meet Peter.

It was just over one hour later that Peter called and was told there were two English girls available. This could be the break they were hoping for. Peter accepted and gave instructions that the girls should come to his hotel at 7 p.m. If one of the English girls turned out to be Kate, they would be able to turn over Claudia's appointment to the Maresciallo who could set an ambush for the meeting on the 10th.

Half an hour later there was yet another call from the answering service, this time for Valerie. She was to go to the hotel designated by Peter at 7 p.m. Everyone breathed a sigh of relief. The situation was beginning to heat up and Roberto decided it was time to call the Maresciallo.

They had been friends for a long time, even so the Maresciallo was quite angry that the Quartet had embarked on such a dangerous course of action. He instructed that under no circumstances was Claudia to keep the appointment. He would deal with everything. However he could not turn down a possible opportunity to locate Kate and agreed that, as there was little risk, they could continue with the arrangements they had made.

By 7 p.m. all four were in the hotel room waiting for the English girl they hoped would be Kate, although Roberto and Claudia remained hidden in the bathroom. The girl arrived five minutes late and from the photographs they had seen, Valerie and Peter instantly recognized her as the ambassador's daughter-in-law. They explained the situation to Kate, who began to panic, fearing that her baby could be at risk. Once they had calmed her, Roberto and Claudia joined the other three and Kate was given the information they had concerning baby Sarah.

They felt confident there was no danger to the baby and told Kate that the urgent concern now was to locate her husband, John, as quickly as possible. Kate then broke down. She had been under tremendous strain for two weeks, not knowing where her daughter or husband were and being compelled to perform acts that were absolutely abhorrent to her.

The next problem was that someone from the agency was due to meet Kate in the foyer of the hotel at 11 p.m. At the appointment she would receive instructions concerning the meeting of the 10th. That information could be vital in tracking down John.

Roberto said there was no way she could return to the agency and after some quick thinking it was agreed she should develop appendicitis and be taken to hospital. That would take her out of circulation for ten days, giving them some time to try to locate John.

The poor girl was in very bad psychological condition and had only been kept going by the promise she had been given, that the family would be reunited after one month. She wasn't convinced but had to keep hope and ultimately had no choice anyway. The hospital idea began to look very promising. She could receive treatment there for her condition resulting from the strain imposed on her by her experiences, while misleading the agency into believing she was there for another reason.

Roberto then came up with yet another suggestion. Kate should demand that the agency permit her to have a visit from her husband while in hospital. Failure to meet her demand would result in her refusal to return to the work that was being forced upon her. She would say as she hadn't seen John in two weeks, for all she knew he could be dead.

At 11 p.m. Valerie was waiting in the foyer with Kate. Claudia, with her expertise in makeup, had given Kate a very pale face and she was doubled up complaining of severe abdominal pains when her contact arrived. He told her she must go with him, he would arrange for a doctor. At that point she feigned loss of consciousness and slumped to the floor. Peter conveniently arrived on the scene claiming he was a doctor and a guest at the hotel.

Peter's act was very convincing and an ambulance was called. As Kate was being lifted into the ambulance she prentended to regain consciousness just long enough to tell the contact that she wished to see her husband. He replied there was nothing he could do but he would report to his boss. He then turned to Valerie and told her she must go with him. Peter would go with Kate to the hospital. He would be able to protect her until the Maresciallo was informed.

Roberto and Claudia were waiting outside the hotel in the BMW, when the contact came hurrying out with Valerie. He virtually threw her into the car, then jumped in and drove off at high speed. Roberto followed at a distance that would hopefully mask the fact. He followed the car up into the hills on the north side of the city where it entered through the gates of a large villa at Rifredi. Roberto turned off his lights and quietly got out of the car, instructing Valerie to call the Maresciallo and let him know the situation.

There was a high wall surrounding the villa which Roberto had to follow for 100 meters or so before finding a suitable tree that would permit him to scale the wall. Once inside the grounds he carefully made his way through the bushes until he reached the lawn in front of the villa. Up to this point the Quartet had been very fortunate in their pseudo detective work. Things were about to change.

Inside the villa a night surveillance camera picked up the figure of a man crossing the lawn and it was not long before Roberto was roughly tied and bundled into a storeroom. Five minutes later the door opened and Valerie was brought in to join him.

"You won't have long to wait. Joe will enjoy finding out what you two are up to. He's very persuasive," Dino sneered as he slammed the door and locked it behind him.

Immediately after receiving Claudia's call the Maresciallo organized a squad and set off for the villa, arriving twenty minutes after Roberto. It was 1 a.m. and a thick fog was rapidly forming in the still, humid air. From the gate it was already impossible to see the villa, which stood on a hill above the road. The Maresciallo didn't want to put Roberto and Valerie into any greater danger and decided to wait for a floor plan of the villa before taking any further action.

Dino went to call Joe DeAntonio and inform him there were two prisoners. By nature Joe was a very angry man and sadistically violent. The day had been difficult for him and he had just managed to get to sleep, consequently Dino was confronted with a stream of abuse when he woke him, though he was accustomed to that and knew it would be much worse in the morning if he had not called Joe.

Joe dressed and he and Dino went to the storeroom where Roberto and Valerie were being held. For a moment Joe studied Roberto, then in a confident voice said,

"I know you, you're Grassina, but who's this lovely thing?" The vision of Valerie woke him up completely. Earlier that evening he had tried to satisfy himself with a young village girl he picked up in a bar. He invariably chose girls of that type and then was not happy with them, finally kicking them out.

Because of his reputation he was never allowed near the girls working for the agency and having Valerie in such a position was a rare opportunity for him to amuse himself with a woman of class. He walked across to where she stood, ran his hand up her skirt and caressed her between the legs very roughly. The touch of her sheer silk stockings was something he was not accustomed to. Roberto was unable to contain himself and jumped up, inflamed with anger and jealousy. His hands were secured behind his back but his feet were free and he succeeded in kicking Joe as hard as he could in the leg.

"Jesus Christ," Joe yelled, as he dropped to the floor grasping his shin. "Shoot that bastard." His face reddened with the intense pain and he moaned and groaned. "I told you to shoot him," he shouted once more at Dino.

In desperation Valerie began to scream at the top of her voice, prompting Dino to grab her and cover her mouth with his hand. Now that she was quiet, he replied to Joe's order.

"Joe, I think you will want to wait when you hear what has happened this evening. We need to interrogate them both."

"OK, but tie his legs." Joe continued to curse the pain and Roberto.

"Listen, lady," Dino warned, "you had better shut up because when Joe gets mad people die, or get very badly hurt."

Valerie did not continue to scream when Dino took his hand from her mouth, instead she decided to try to invoke the force she had had in France a week before. Now that Valerie was quiet Dino walked across to where Roberto stood and threw him to the floor. He then secured his legs with rope and lifted him back onto the chair. Now that Roberto was imobilized, Joe hobbled across, drew back his right arm and punched Roberto in the mouth with all his force. The impact was substantial and Valerie saw blood spurt from Roberto's mouth as he tumbled over, his head striking the floor with a dull thud. Valerie's heart jumped a beat when she saw Roberto lying still on the floor. Joe now felt more secure and turned his attention once more to Valerie.

"Look, I don't care what has happened tonight, first I am going to have this one."

Valerie went cold with fear, try though she may all the concentration she could summon had produced no effect whatever. Now some ugly, filthy beast was about to use her like a whore.

"Boss, listen, the English dame is gone."

Joe spun round, his eyes glaring at Dino.

"What do you mean she's gone?"

"When I went to pick her up at the hotel she was looking terrible, all white and doubled up with pain. She said she needed a doctor. I told her she must come back here and that we would get a doctor for her, then she fainted and some foreign doctor, staying in the hotel, said she was close to peritonitis and called for an ambulance. There was nothing I could do."

"Right. You keep this bitch quiet. I am going to make a couple of phone calls."

Valerie felt a temporary sense of relief as Joe left the room, but she was very concerned about Roberto who continued to remain still on the floor, blood seeping slowly from the corner of his mouth.

"Listen, lady, I am warning you, you had better do as Joe tells you. He doesn't mess about and always gets his way."

"OK. I will do as I am told but please have a look at him."

Dino bent down and checked the pulse in Roberto's neck.

"He'll be all right, he just had a bit of a knock on the ...."

At that moment Roberto swung his legs in a wide, rapid arc knocking Dino's legs away from under him. He came crashing to the floor alongside Roberto who instantly swung his tied feet once more, this time striking the man precisely on the chin. Dino emitted one muted "Uh" then became quiet.

"Let's get out of here," Roberto whispered to Valerie. "Quickly untie me."

In a matter of seconds Roberto was free and they hurried along the corridor to the back entrance of the villa. There Valerie was able to open the door which they both hurtled through, tumbling down a flight of steps, a rude introduction to the dense fog.

"My God," Valerie moaned, " are you all right?"

"I think so. I am sure we both have many bruises, but I can't believe this fog. I've seen fog many times around Florence. It is almost a permanent feature here during the winter months, but nothing like this. How about you, no serious damage?"

"My arm is broken."

"Hold on. I'm coming across."

Roberto had thirty-two years' experience of finding things in the dark. His foot gently touched Valerie.

"That's you," he said confidently.

"Yes, that's my leg. I am afraid the fracture is compound. I can feel the bone sticking out and the arm is in a very strange position. At the moment I can feel almost nothing but it's only a matter of time before it is going to become very painful."

"I will apologize for getting you into this once we are out of it," Roberto promised. "For the moment, somehow, you are going to have to be very strong."

At that instant the outside lights of the villa were switched on, though they did almost nothing, being smothered by the fog. Then came the unmistakable sound of a shotgun being cocked.

Roberto and Valerie struggled to their feet, without a word. He held her good arm and they lunged headlong into the grey swirling mist. Behind them they heard the sound of someone descending the steps, then came the first sound of a shot, causing Roberto and Valerie to drop to the ground and lay as low and still as they could. They were just in time before a series of pairs of shots rang out in all direction, with a short delay for reloading in between. Then a second gunman joined the shooting escapade, probably Dino. The pair felt reasonably safe on the ground, nevertheless the constant barrage of shots was very frightening. Apparently the gunmen had decided to just shoot in all directions in the hope of getting lucky.

At the gates of the villa the shots were also heard by the Maresciallo, who decided it necessary to take some action. He felt it was reasonable to make his presence known and grabbing a megaphone from the car he announced that the carabinieri had surrounded the villa and that the shooting should stop.

Roberto and Valerie heard the voice of the Maresciallo and were surprised that the firing did in fact cease. The air became eerily quiet and they had the feeling of being in a very small world, the fog and darkness combining to create just the space that held them.

"Come on," Roberto whispered, "let's try to make our way toward the sound we just heard."

Valerie's arm was beginning to throb and the pain was growing by the minute. She wanted to scream out but could not. Roberto held her hand firmly so they should not be separated in the fog. They had an advantage over their pursuers in that they had both experienced blindness and therefore were able to deal with the circumstances in which they found themselves much more readily, a fact that occurred to them both and gave them a certain amount of confidence.

Soon they heard the sound of conversation in the near distance and felt the smooth level surface of an asphalt road under their feet. Neither called out, they just continued their steady progress.

A couple of minutes later they reached the gates, which were locked. It would be impossible for Valerie to climb the gates with her broken arm, in addition to which the pain had become very intense, making it urgent that she receive medical attention.

Roberto told the Maresciallo to bring one of the cars as near to the gates as possible. He then followed the wires leading to the electronic gate release back to a junction box and yanked the wires out of the box. Next he stripped the ends with his teeth and instructed the Maresciallo to touch the bare ends to the car battery.

"No, don't worry about polarity, it is just a solenoid."

The visibility at the gate was very poor but not so restricted as at the villa, making it possible to carry out the exercise without the risk of being seen by DeAntonio or Dino.

Roberto had been right. The supply to the gate was twelve volts and as the bare wires made contact with the car battery the sound of the gate release mechanism could be heard.

Roberto pulled open the massive wrought iron gate and led Valerie out to the car, where Claudia helped her in. Claudia told Roberto she would take Valerie to the hospital if he wished to remain.

"No, I am coming too" he said. "There appear to be only two men in the villa," he shouted back to the Maresciallo as they drove away. "One is very vicious. I will call you on the car phone as we drive to the city and fill you in."

Claudia maintained the highest speed possible in the fog that was intensifying by the minute, although the visibility became better as they reached the bottom of the hill.

Roberto held Valerie's hand in an attempt to soothe her, as he telephoned the Maresciallo. While he spoke he saw the tears of pain beginning to run down her face and felt his intestines knotting up at the sight of the woman he loved in such agony as a result of being involved in his problems; despite which he was obliged to maintain his calm and explain to the Maresciallo everything that had happened during the course of the evening.

They arrived at the Ospedale Santa Maria Nuova near the cathedral, the same hospital where Peter had taken Kate a couple of hours before. The 'Pronto Soccorso',

(Emergency Room), jumped into action immediately. Firstly Valerie was given a shot to ease the pain, then a surgeon was called.

Once Valerie was wheeled into the operating theatre Roberto hurried to the inquiry desk to ask where he could find Peter and Kate. He was instructed to wait while the doctor who was dealing with her case was called.

The receptionist had been instructed to call the two carabinieri officers, should anyone ask for Kate, and shortly they arrived, both with weapons trained on Roberto. As they drew close one of the officers recognized Roberto, advised the other, and they lowered their weapons.

"Excuse us, sir," one of them said, "we are expecting that someone from the agency might try to get to the young lady."

Apparently Peter had taken the girl back to *Il Palazzo* and was waiting there to hear from Roberto, who instantly called him and gave him the news concerning Valerie.

"Peter, has Kate settled down yet?" There was a brief pause, "OK, I think it would be best if you bring her back here to the hospital. Another pause, "Yes, the one by the cathedral. Fine, see you soon."

Roberto then hurried back to wait outside the operating theatre.

Everything now depended on the police. Hopefully they would be able to locate John with the new information to hand, then reunite the couple. Once that was achieved they could concentrate on tracking down baby Sarah in Florida.

When Valerie was finally wheeled out of the operating theatre, she was accompanied by the surgeon, who told Roberto that although it had been a compound fracture, the break was clean and the resetting had been quite straightforward. She could now return home.

Claudia, Peter, and Kate had arrived in the meantime and there was a general sense of relief that they were all together once more.

Roberto explained that Kate would have to remain in the hospital. There would be police protection for her and she would be given treatment for her psychological condition. The others would return to *Il Palazzo*.

It was 4 a.m. when, with the exception of Valerie, who was resting, they assembled in the 'operations room' to analyze the day's information.

Roberto confessed he was very concerned for John and the baby. He explained that while he and Valerie were held captive in the villa at Rifredi, Joe DeAntonio had made telephone calls concerning the fact that Kate was no longer with the agency. The only hope was that they had accepted she was in hospital with appendicitis. Whatever, they agreed they didn't think there was a real danger to the child. John was the one most likely to be used for blackmail in the circumstances.

"I think we should all get just a few hours sleep," Roberto suggested. "Let's see what tomorrow brings. With a bit of luck the meeting will still proceed, despite the fact that Claudia didn't keep her appointment."

"We will have to keep Claudia under continuous protection," Peter cautioned. "The organization will not be happy and will surely try to get to her."

The previous day had been long with intense activity, consequently all were extremely tired and it was around 9 a.m. the following morning that a telephone call from the Maresciallo disturbed Roberto's sleep.

Having replaced the receiver, he told Valerie that Joe DeAntonio and Dino had been arrested and were currently being interrogated. There was a great deal of evidence at the villa and every aspect of the evidence was being investigated with all possible speed. The police appreciated the potential danger to John in the present circumstances. During the night there had been a telephone call to the hospital. The caller had been told that Kate had had an operation and was in recovery. She could not be disturbed. He persisted that he was her husband and wished to see her as soon as possible, in answer to which the hospital said he could visit her during the afternoon at 5 p.m.

There was little likelihood that the caller had been John, and an ambush would be set.

Valerie insisted she wished to be included in the meeting after breakfast. She had something important to tell everyone concerning a dream she had had. The four were assembled and anxious to hear the details, as they all had great confidence in Valerie's dreams. Valerie began to recount the details.

"I saw a cargo ship. It was moored at a port with a very long name which I cannot remember, although I am sure I would recognize it if I heard it again."

"Civitavecchia," Roberto exclaimed.

"Yes, that was it, but how could you know so quickly?" Valerie queried.

"My belief is that you are going to say the dream involved John," Roberto asserted. "I also believe he is being used by the organization in activity related to drugs. Civitavecchia is a major port near Rome and the most likely to be used in the shipment of drugs."

"You must be inheriting mystic abilities," Valerie replied. She then continued, "In my dream I saw a man holding a packet. With his finger he was sampling and tasting what was in the packet. He then looked up at another man, whom I recognized from the photographs as John, and said, "OK, it is now 2 a.m. Saturday morning. Be here tomorrow at the same time and I will have the cash." What do you think, should we go to Civitavecchia?"

"Well, today is Friday," Roberto said. "Let's hope your dream related to the day after tomorrow and not last Sunday. Yes, I think we should go to Civitavecchia. Were there any other details in your dream?"

"No, I'm afraid not."

The day of the funeral of Edoardo, Eleanora, and Gina had arrived. At 11 a.m. the Quartet would attend the service. They must now set aside all other matters until after the family were laid to rest.

Six

The day began serenely, a huge splash of orange lighting up the eastern sky as the sun rose. Then gradually the orange submitted to an ever more azure blue.

Throughout the 400-year history of *Il Palazzo* there had never been such a tragic series of incidents as those resulting in the triple funeral that was about to take place.

The mourners moved around the palace and grounds in their somber yet elegant attire, talking in subdued tones, reflecting on what a beautiful family it had been, that was now gone. There was a general feeling of numbness; the horror so intense as to be unacceptable to the mind.

In the private chapel of the palace the still bodies of Edoardo, Eleanora and Gina lay in open coffins, a continuous line of mourners passing by, paying their last respects. Those staying at the palace were joined by yet more distant relatives and friends, together with well-wishers from the surrounding area, all giving homage to those whose lives had been so brutally terminated.

Just before 11 a.m., Roberto and Claudia led Peter and Valerie down the aisle of cold grey stone, with dark, ancient, hand-carved pews to left and right. When they reached the coffins they stood with their heads bowed, like a guard of honor, gazing with distant eyes into the satin-lined boxes. For a while time stood still. There were no thoughts of how the tragedy had occurred, no recriminations, no blame, just a very deep feeling of loss and profound sadness. The scene was almost unbearable and each of the four found it impossible to suppress their tears. Then they moved to their places and stood in silent prayer.

The closest members of the family began to file into the chapel and the seats, that had been assembled on the grass in front of the entrance to accommodate those who could not find a seat in the small but holy place, were also completely occupied within a short period of time.

The Bishop conducted the ceremony, as he had promised, skillfully masking the fact that he had not actually consecrated the coffin of Edoardo and, in another place, the Carini family were also saying their last farewells to Don Carini and his previously unknown son Giulio. Ironically, because Don Carini had been murdered before he had the opportunity to carry out his intended suicide, *his* funeral proceeded as for any good Catholic, despite the life he had led, the final judgment being left to his maker.

Edoardo's action had had a negative effect; however, even knowing the potential repercussions, he had died with a certain satisfaction, knowing that the man who had, however inadvertently, been responsible for the deaths of his wife and daughter, had died by his hand. He had tried very hard to suppress his anger but the loss was so great that he felt life held nothing more for him and he could not leave while Carini was still living.

For a few hours the Quartet immersed themselves in the sadness of the day.

By 4 p.m. most of the guests who were not staying at the palace had left and Roberto decided it was time for them to prepare their strategy for the evening. Time was limited and there was hope that something good could come about on a day that should not have happened.

They learned that Claudia's appointment for the previous evening had been kept by an undercover policewoman. When the 'client' arrived at the hotel room, it transpired he was a high-ranking politician and the police had no problem in securing his word that he would behave as though the rendezvous had been quite normal.

During the evening a contact had arrived, as arranged, and left details of the monthly meeting, though on this occasion it would be Claudia in person who would have to attend because the Madame, and a number of other members of the agency, had seen her. The police would prepare an ambush and were confident there was no danger for her.

Peter did his best to convince Claudia not to keep the appointment but in the end conceded that the potential gain far outweighed the risk. As a precaution he provided her with the electronic bug.

The meeting had been set for 6 p.m., probably so as to avoid clashing with any client appointments. Claudia drove herself to the designated house in a car provided by police. On her arrival at the old, converted, isolated farmhouse, she was shown through to a large downstairs reception room that had probably been a stable in days gone by.

She expected there would be other girls already at the house and became concerned when she entered the room and found herself to be alone. After fifteen anxious minutes, during which time no one else appeared, a stocky woman entered the room and as soon as she began to speak Claudia recognized her voice as that of the Madame.

"Claudia, it is you. Well, I must say your brother caused us a great deal of trouble yesterday evening. Yes, I know who you are. Claudia Grassina."

The microphone picked up clearly the words uttered by the Madame and on hearing them Roberto immediately started up the BMW and began to move in the direction of the farmhouse. Peter became very agitated, his protective instinct urged him to rush headlong into whatever the situation, in defence of the woman he loved.

It would seem that Joe had been very astute and when he made his calls the evening before, the agency had been able to establish a connection and finally realized who Claudia was.

"I am here merely to confirm your identity," the Madame continued. "From here you will be taken to one of our 'special' houses. It will give me great pleasure to explain what will happen to you there. If one of our girls disobeys the rules she is also taken to a 'special' house. There, like you, she is used to help satisfy the demand we have for babies for adoption. You will be comfortable and well looked after but of course you will never be permitted to leave."

Roberto continued to drive while he made contact with the Maresciallo. They discussed the unexpected and worrying development and Roberto said he hoped there would be an opportunity to intercept the car transporting Claudia.

Then came the voice of the Madame once more,

"By the way, Claudia, we anticipated the police may be nearby. Movement has already been noted. We are not so stupid; however, they will not present a problem. This old house has a very unique feature. It was originally part of the estate of one of the Dukes of Tuscany. He had many enemies and introduced an escape route, dug by six hundred of his prisoners. The tunnel took two years to complete and the prisoners who did not die in the terrible conditions in which they were expected to work, were killed so that no one would know the secret of the passage-way."

Peter suggested that if the tunnel were of any substantial length, ventilator shafts would be necessary and would appear at intervals on the surface. Roberto stopped the car approximately 500 meters short of the farmhouse, where, together with Valerie and Peter, he began to visually scan the fields around the house looking for any signs of possible vent holes.

"Unfortunately, once they are underground we will lose the signal from the bug," Peter continued. Previously being able to monitor any movement or dialogue had given them a certain degree of confidence. Once that contact was lost things would change dramatically. Everyone started to become very nervous and concerned for Claudia.

From their new position the three were able to see that the police surrounding the house were beginning to close in.

Then Claudia's bug picked up the voice of a man.

"It is time for us to leave. I suggest you do exactly as you are told, Claudia. You are useful to us but if you become a liability I will shoot you instantly."

For a couple of minutes there were sounds of hurried footsteps, then a creaking noise, probably a door being opened, then silence.

A helicopter was already standing by in the area and Roberto called the Maresciallo once more.

"We believe there should be some vent holes for the tunnel," Roberto conveyed Peter's suggestion. "If the pilot flies in ever-increasing circles around the farmhouse maybe he will see something."

The Maresciallo agreed and instructed the pilot accordingly.

It was not long before the pilot radioed that he had located what appeared to be a vent hole, approximately 150 meters southwest of the farm. By then it was 6:45 p.m. and the light was fading as the sun began to sink toward the horizon, lighting the sky with the same massive orange glow in the west that in the morning had coloured the eastern sky.

Roberto instantly veered off the road, smashing through the hedge and into a field. The field was strewn with small rocks that constantly impacted the underside of the car and even the luxury BMW was unable to compensate for the violent and erratic jolts caused by the irregular terrain.

They had been on the east side of the farmhouse and were now driving directly toward the setting sun, adding a further hazard to their progress.

Roberto was concerned for Valerie, who assured him that her arm was quite comfortable and egged him on, in response to which Roberto pressed the accelerator pedal still lower. Then, when they arrived at a point some 200 meters southwest of the house, Roberto suddenly slammed on the brakes, causing the vehicle to come to a violent stop just a few centimeters from the edge of a rift. A cloud of dust swirled around the car and cut off their vision completely for a minute or so and as the extraneous noises came to an abrupt halt the Maresciallo's voice could be heard shouting that they should stop. The pilot had seen the car approaching the sudden drop in the ground and was fearful of the potential consequences. He relayed the information to the Maresciallo who in turn tried to warn Roberto.

"We're OK. I saw the gap just in time. "

The dust dropped like a curtain and as the rift came into full view they saw that a car was parked at the base of one of the slopes. They were at the closed end and Roberto decided to follow the edge at a speed that did not create too much dust. He also suggested to the Maresciallo that the helicopter move away from the area. It was important to create the impression that the escape had been successful, thereby reducing the risk to Claudia.

Roberto pacified Peter by saying that if there had been any intention of harming Claudia it would have happened already. For the moment it might be wise to ease back on the chase and allow them to escape, while constantly maintaining them under surveillance. If they tried to intercept the car the risk to Claudia could be even greater.

Peter wished to have Claudia back in his arms as soon as possible but after a moment of careful consideration he agreed that it was probably in her best interest to let them reach their destination believing they had evaded the police.

Roberto stopped the car and explained their feelings to the Maresciallo over the car phone. He agreed. And quickly it was arranged that a relay of cars would follow the car carrying Claudia, by which method they would hope the Madame and whoever else was in the car with Claudia would not realize they were being tailed.

The helicopter was instructed to return to base, having given details of the roads that gave access to the exit of the rift. Then the Maresciallo sent three of his unmarked cars to drive slowly in an outward direction from the access road. Shortly the message came back that one of the cars had been passed by a silver Fiat 132 in which Claudia and her captors had been seen. They were travelling in a northeasterly direction towards Forli.

As Roberto heard the details he turned the BMW in a heading that would bring them to the same road. Soon they were driving through the Alpe di San Benedetto, a series of small mountain ranges reaching up to 3500 ft.

The signal from the miniature transmitter Claudia was carrying was being picked up by the police radios also and it became possible to pinpoint the location of the Fiat by using two different points of reception and intercepting on a map the angles of strongest signal. Occasionally the signal would be lost because of the terrain but Peter became a little more relaxed as the Fiat continued to move at a steady speed.

There was almost no conversation in the Fiat until Claudia decided to make a comment concerning Sarah. She apparently decided to try to give them the impression the police thought the baby was still in Italy, thus giving them a false sense of security.

"You realize that the baby you kidnapped two weeks ago is the grand-daughter of a diplomat. It will be impossible for you to transport the baby out of Italy."

"Claudia," the Madame replied, "our organization is very sophisticated. There is no possibility that the police could locate the child."

"That's enough," a male voice snapped. "No talking."

The journey continued on beyond Forli where the car picked up the A14 going south. They had left the mountains behind and there was no further loss of signal from the bug across the undulating terrain.

It was almost 10 p.m. when they reached the outskirts of Rimini and the pace slowed. On the coast road they became immersed in the evening traffic of holiday-makers and began to fear they might lose contact, until the Fiat turned on to a small road that led to the beach.

At the end of the road was a high fence approximately 30 meters long where the car came to a stop. From some way back Roberto and the other two saw Claudia leave the car with a short woman, who was probably the Madame, and two men. They went through a gate, walked up to the house and went in.

"We must act tonight," Peter said anxiously. "I'm not going to just ..."

The car phone interrupted Peter and Roberto answered. After the call he told the other two that the Maresciallo was parked just 50 meters behind them. He had decided, like Peter, that it was urgent to get Claudia out as quickly as possible. Reinforcements would arrive in about fifteen minutes and when they did Roberto would receive another call telling him where they were to congregate.

The call came just ten minutes later, though it seemed like hours, particularly for Peter who was unaccustomed to waiting, being a man of action.

"Come on," Roberto said and began to leave the car, then stuck his head back inside. "How about you, Valerie, do you want to come? You can rest in the car if you wish." Before he could even finish speaking Valerie was on the pavement,

"I am with you," she replied.

They found the large van parked just around the corner and everyone was invited in by the Maresciallo who turned to Roberto and said,

"It is thanks to you three that we have arrived at this point, but I am afraid I must ask you to leave the next stage to us."

Peter stated his desire to be involved. "My only concern is for Claudia," he assured the Maresciallo. "You will be concentrating on arresting whoever is there. If you will permit me to join you I give you my word that I will follow your instructions without query, and take responsibility for Claudia when the time comes."

The Maresciallo thought for a moment, then with a grin agreed that if it was his fiance being held he would also wish to be there.

"Yes, you may come. Excuse me, Roberto, I must be firm. No one else."

"OK," Roberto replied.

"The way I see it," the Maresciallo continued, "we are tired from the journey, so are they. They think the day is over and has been successful, which will hopefully mean they are off their guard. We will wait till 3 a.m. The building fronts onto the beach and there are many security cameras; however, it is a very dark night and we have a special squad that will come in from the sea."

The plan was prepared with considerable intelligence and common sense and everyone was confident the operation would be a success.

In the couple of hours before the police operation was due to begin the Maresciallo invited the trio to join him and the local chief of police for a meal.

They found a restaurant still open and after a long day, without time to eat, everything tasted delicious, except to Peter who was too anxious to eat. During the meal they discussed all the developments relating to the ambassador's family and arrangements were made to send a fax to Bucharest with the latest news.

The time arrived. It had already been discovered that the fence around the building was electrified, and an emergency power crew had been brought in to deactivate it. The cameras were still a problem, although, Peter confirmed, with the aid of night vision binoculars provided by the police, he had been able to study the types of cameras used and was confident they were not low-light cameras, consequently they would only be useful once the outside lights were on.

Valerie and Roberto, having returned to the BMW, had an almost uninterrupted view of the house and they strained their eyes in an endeavor to catch sight of what was going on.

It was not even 3:05 a.m. when lights suddenly started to be switched on all over the building, followed by several shots, then all was quiet.

Roberto and Valerie gained the impression it was over and cautiously left the car, walking slowly toward the house. When they were just short of the fence the front door of the building suddenly burst open and there stood Peter with his arm firmly around Claudia. Both were waving furiously and as the couples drew closer to each other they all had beaming smiles on their faces. Soon there was a confusion of arms and bodies. The Quartet were once again united.

It was 3:15 a.m. and they were a long drive from Florence, but before setting off on the return journey they went into the house with the intention of debriefing with the Maresciallo. What they found, when they met up with the police in the main hallway, was a collection of young, attractive women in various stages of pregnancy. That could have been Claudia's fate, they thought. The Madame and six or seven other people, who were evidently members of the group, were being handcuffed and led out to a waiting police van.

Roberto walked across to the Maresciallo, took his hand in a firm shake and thanked him very sincerely for what he had done in making it possible to rescue his sister. Peter had already tendered his thanks. The four then excused themselves to begin the journey back to Florence. In less than twenty-four hours they needed to be in Civitavecchia on the Mediterranean, a long and difficult drive from their present position on the Adriatic coast.

Seven

By the time they pulled into the port of Civitavecchia no one had been able to get more than six hours sleep. The last 150 km had been undertaken in torrential rain and the temperature had dropped dramatically since they left Rimini. Under the street lights the roads were black and shiny as huge TIR (tractor trailer trucks), thundered in both directions, ever more frequent as they approached the docks. Sheets of water thrown up by the 18-wheelers temporarily cut off vision for whoever was driving at the time, adding to the tension.

The lack of sleep and poor driving conditions saw the four with red eyes and strained nerves. Even their morale had dropped, despite the success they had already achieved in finding Kate. Each was silently thinking maybe Valerie's dream would have no foundation this time and the journey would prove fruitless. Even if the dream had been a prophetic vision maybe it related to a different Sunday, added to which the docks were massive. Where to start?

Since their arrival in Italy Valerie had experienced only two small occurrences of her mystic premonitions. The information in her dream, that had caused them to make the long drive to Civitavecchia, contained no detail and Valerie was just hoping that being in the location of her dream might prompt some further clues. She felt very responsible. If they found nothing it would mean they had invested a great deal of effort for nothing. On the other hand, for the moment it was all they had to go on.

The docks operated on a twenty-four hour schedule and there was a great deal of activity, with many ships from all over the world loading and unloading. At the harbour-master's office Valerie was taken to the operations center, where closed circuit cameras monitored the entire area.

For ten minutes Valerie scanned from one monitor to another, paying particular attention to ships plying between ports known for a history of drug activity. Suddenly she realized she was concentrating on one monitor, though that particular picture was very indistinct.

"The ship is from Venezuela." The words came from her mouth in that monosyllabic tone, as she stared at the small screen. "Inside one of the crew cabins the man who was with John is filling a blue duffel bag with small packets, similar to those I saw before."

"How do you know that?" the harbour-master asked with a very surprised look on his face.

"I will explain later," Roberto replied for Valerie. "We must go quickly to where that ship is moored."

"Come with me," the harbour-master called as he hurried out of the door and down the stairs to his jeep. The five climbed into the vehicle and sped off toward the north end of the docks. While he drove the harbour-master alerted the harbour police and arranged to meet up with a squad in a building adjacent to where the ship was tied up.

They parked inside one of the huge storage sheds and ran the full length of the building to the end facing the ship, once more inspired with new confidence.

The security guard in the shed had been notified of their impending arrival and was keeping an eye on his monitors while waiting for them. As they arrived he indicated the monitor highlighting the ship from Venezuela. It was in almost total darkness, just a ghostly outline on the screen, and there was no activity around her. Everyone strained their eyes for any sign of movement while the harbour police team continued to arrive.

The group was assembled by 12:45 a.m. and took up positions where any suspicious new arrivals could be intercepted or unusual movement on the ship's decks observed. Valerie remained with her eyes fixed on the monitor.

The vessel had finished unloading the day before and the cranes that had been delving into her holds stood quiet, casting great shadows along the dock from the powerful lights illuminating the ships fore and aft.

By 1 a.m. the regular traffic moving to and fro along the dock side included representatives from the harbour police, wearing stevedore clothing over their uniforms. Everything looked perfectly normal. The trap was set.

At 1:45 a.m., a car drew up in front of the building and the lights were switched off. A camera on the corner of the building was panned into position so that everyone could see the car on one of the monitors. Unfortunately the lights and shadows were not helpful and it was impossible to make out whether or not the occupant of the car was John: however, something was beginning to happen that seemed to give credence to Valerie's dream.

They agreed not to take any action immediately and sure enough, ten minutes later, someone began to move on the deck of the ship. The figure came to the gunwales and briefly flashed a light onto the parked car. For a long three minutes there was no further movement, then the car door opened and the driver went to the rear of the car, opened the trunk and took out a duffel bag. He then walked over to the gang-way leading up onto the deck and began to climb the suspended, swaying structure.

Valerie became quite excited.

"That's the bag I saw in my dream," she exclaimed.

Shortly the man on deck could be seen moving toward the top of the gang-plank, evidently to receive the bag. As he passed through a narrow shaft of light he was seen to be apparently screwing a silencer onto the muzzle of a revolver. He stopped at the entrance to the gang-plank and waited, by which time the other man, presumed to be John, had arrived halfway up and obviously could not have seen what was going on above him.

Before reaching the top, the man on the gang-plank passed through the same shaft of light that had previously highlighted the pistol on deck. From the photographs the Quartet had seen there was no doubt that it was John and once it was confirmed the harbour-master instructed that floodlights be switched on to illuminate the area. The harbour police then made their presence known as they converged from all directions. John, fearing being involved in a drug arrest, began to run to the top of the plank and as he did so a single shot rang out from an upstairs window of the building. The man on deck fell and made no further signs of movement.

When he arrived on deck John ran across to the other side of the ship. He was seen to stuff the duffel bag under the tarpaulin cover of one of the life boats, a desperate act, then he clambered up onto the gunwales and jumped over the side into the sea.

Peter and Roberto ran outside where the sound of motorboat engines being started could be heard. Peter, who had run to the bow of the ship, was also seen to jump into the water.

Valerie and Claudia joined Roberto just in front of the bow of the ship where two harbour policemen were directing the beams of flashlights into the dark, murky water. The flashlights picked out Peter struggling with John, who was desperately trying to get away. Whenever they were on the surface Peter could be heard trying to complete a sentence that Kate was now under police protection and was well. Finally the message got through and a couple of minutes later the two were being helped onto a small boat that had arrived on the scene.

Morning newspapers, radio, and TV carried the story of a drug bust in which both the buyer and seller had been shot dead and a large sum of money, together with a consignment of crack cocaine, seized. There were photographs of the two dead men, John putting on a very convincing act.

The whole operation had taken a little over thirty minutes, and now it was over everyone, except John, was anxious to sleep, long and deep. The Quartet found a hotel, while John was taken by the police, quite happy to be in their company, to police headquarters where his first desire was to speak with Kate. She was still undergoing treatment and the hospital was called. The majority of the Italian police in the room did not understand what John was saying but there was no doubt about the look of happiness on his face and tears of joy running down his cheeks.

The following morning a police helicopter flew John to Florence, while the Quartet left later by car, their destination being *Il Palazzo*.

Neither John nor Kate had been physically injured but the psychological damage to both was very deep. When they were finally reunited, the following day, their embraces were so intense as to almost join them into one being. It could be imagined that John would never let Kate out of his sight again. There remained one very delicate and difficult problem to overcome, finding baby Sarah.

The arrival of the BMW at *Il Palazzo*, later in the afternoon, conflicted the existing and continued air of sadness with the satisfaction of rescuing John and Kate, who were also awaiting the arrival of the Quartet.

During the morning the young couple had been almost constantly on the telephone. They called the ambassador, in Bucharest, John's mother and to Kate's family in northern Ireland.

Roberto decided to have a banquet to honor the couple and to celebrate their freedom. He assured them it was just a matter of time before their baby would be back in their arms. He also felt that the function would go some way toward helping improve the atmosphere at the palace, where everyone was still reeling from the deaths of Edoardo and his family.

Valerie had given up the east bedroom to the couple to complete their joy and even though they were still separated from their daughter they had almost been reborn. The success achieved by the Quartet in bringing them together gave them the confidence that they would soon have their baby back with them and they were happy to leave Roberto to head the search.

Eight

Monday morning. After a good night's rest, the air of panic had subsided and the members of the Quartet were all completely relaxed after enduring several nights with little sleep.

In the *camera del est* Kate and John were trying to come to terms with the terrible acts they had both been compelled to commit.

Initially, once they were alone in the glorious luxury of the most beautiful room in the palace, the longing for each other, that had grown over the two weeks they were apart, was satisfied with an orgy of love-making followed by satisfied peaceful sleep.

The following morning John, who was an excessively jealous man, relished the memories of the night before with the woman he loved so desperately. She had been a magnificent lover. Different, much more experienced than before. The variations she had employed, that had given him such pleasure and roused him to the ultimate heights, he realized, she must have also performed for other men while they were apart.

Had she enjoyed being a whore for other men? The thought tortured and tortured him until finally he could stand it no longer.

"When you were with other men di ...."

"Please, John, we are together now. I love you very much and I am happy. I just want my baby to make the world complete and perfect."

"Kate, you know I love you too, it is just that last night you were different. It was wonderful, but the things you did, how did you learn them?"

Kate knew how possessive and jealous John was and knew that whatever she said he would not be satisfied and would be convinced she had enjoyed the encounters she had been obliged to participate in.

"John, we must be sure from the beginning. I can swear to you that I felt dirty. What I had to do was totally abhorrent to me but if you are not going to accept my word we must consider our futures and that of our child, otherwise there is the danger that all three of us will live miserable lives."

Kate had tried to clear the air; unfortunately, to John, the words had a totally different meaning. For him she was saying she wanted to separate. Obviously among the men she had been with, one or maybe several had meant more to her than he. Every moment of the two weeks he had suffered, had been involved with drugs, drugs that two years ago had taken the life of his best friend. He had done those things for Kate and the baby. For her the whole time had been nothing but pleasure, a never-ending period of sex and love-making. She probably hadn't even thought of him.

He grabbed her shoulders in a steel grip that gave her considerable pain and his eyes burnt into hers as he shouted,

"What have you done?"

"John, please, you are hurting me. I have done nothing that I wanted to do. Each time I was raped, I had pain. I was forced to be with ugly, disgusting old men." Thank God they were ugly, John thought. "All I could think of was you and our baby. I had no idea where you were, or even if you were alive. It was so terrible that I felt I never wanted another man to touch me or even look at me again. Then last night when you held me I was able to forget a little of what I had been through. You were wonderful and I loved being with you. That is because I love you. I love you more now than I have ever loved you, something I thought impossible before."

John released his grip on her and sank to the floor on his knees,

"Please forgive me," he begged, "you know how these terrible rages of jealousy come over me. I cannot bear to think of anyone touching you. I know you didn't want it. Oh, Kate, I am so sorry."

His eyes became glassy as he tried to hold back the tears and planted a firm salty kiss on her full lips. She held his head in both her hands and massaged his scalp.

"Shoosh, you know I understand. We must be so grateful we are together once more. Without the help of these wonderful people we had, perhaps, only a short time to live. We must both try to forget what has happened. That is impossible, of course, but we have our whole lives ahead of us now. That is God's gift to us. Just love me and stay with me every moment, then we will be happy once more. It just needs time to heal a little."

John dried his eyes and vowed to himself that he would never behave that way again. Kate was a charming, beautiful, and caring wife and he was a very fortunate man.

The hands that had been so rough, just a moment ago, became gentle as he ran his fingers softly up and down her spine. Slowly he opened her blouse and began to press his lips on her breasts. He encircled first one nipple then the other in gentle kisses.

There came a knock on the door and the voice of Roberto, tentatively enquiring if they would like to have tea sent to the room or if they would be coming down for breakfast.

"You are very kind," John replied. "We will be down in twenty minutes."

"Fine. Just make your way to the dining room."

The interruption brought them back to reality.

"Let's dress and go down. I promise I will never speak of it again," John swore as he kissed her once more and closed her blouse.

The Quartet had finished their breakfast when John and Kate appeared; however, Roberto was waiting for them and told John that the police had called and were very anxious to interview him. He could give them a great deal of intelligence concerning the drug deals he had been involved in.

Kate was also expected back at the hospital. The psychologist who had been attending her had telephoned, wishing to know when she intended to return.

"Listen. Today we are preparing a banquet in your honor and we would be very pleased to have you both here for the day. What do you think?"

John looked at Kate and they smiled at one another.

"We would love that," Kate replied. "But you have done so much for us already."

"No problem, it is our pleasure. Tomorrow the four of us are leaving for Florida where we intend to commence the hunt for Sarah."

"I cannot believe that there are such wonderful people in the world. I had come to think that everyone was evil," Kate said, a new joy filling her heart.

John got up from his chair and walked across to where Roberto sat, extended his hand, which Roberto took, and shaking it firmly said, "I thank you so much for giving me Kate and rescuing us both. That would have been more than anyone could ask. That it will be the four of you looking for our Sarah gives us absolute confidence. You will find her and bring her back to us, I know."

The handshake continued for a moment beyond John's declaration, then John returned to his seat as Roberto began to speak once more.

"I haven't had the chance to tell you both what we have discovered so far. In Florida we located five adoption agencies that appear to be more interested in finances than finding a good home for any children that are their responsibility. We will begin by contacting them. We have also been informed, this morning, that the international criminal who delivered Sarah to Florida has an alligator farm in the middle of the state. We intend to try to bring him to justice also. Apparently he has not left the U.S.A. and although, for the moment, the police have no reason to question him, they have promised to keep him under observation."

"That's fantastic," Kate said excitedly, as she squeezed John's hand.

"Well, if you will excuse me now I have things to attend to. We will meet again later." Roberto left the room and Kate and John began their breakfast with new hope.

It became Roberto's problem to make arrangements for the banquet. Thoughts of Edoardo had not left him for a moment, even so the task brought back memories of the previous ten years when it had always been Edoardo who attended to the functions at the palace. Now he was no longer there, his skill and care in making such preparations would be sorely missed. Roberto began to brood on thoughts of Edoardo and he became more and more depressed, until Valerie appeared.

"I have come to help with the preparations for this evening. What can I do?"

"Dear Valerie, you arrived just in time to take me out of myself. I was just thinking how Edoardo always took responsibility for the social events held at the palace, then the bulk of my concentration shifted to the fact that he is gone. Edoardo would not want things that way. He will be here, in spirit, helping us. Come on, let's go and talk to chef Luigi."

Roberto and Valerie spent the better part of the morning preparing for the evening while Claudia and Peter concentrated on the next day and their departure for Florida.

The evening soiree was indeed a grand affair, designed to raise the spirits of the family and revel in the success of the Quartet in bringing about the rescue of John and Kate.

Once all the guests were assembled in '*Il Salotto Grande*' Roberto called for silence and said a prayer for Edoardo, Eleanora and Gina. As the prayer finished, and before the guests had the opportunity to sink into melancholy, a fanfare sounded from a gallery above one end of the massive room, the mirrored doors swung open and John and Kate were led into the room. They were a very handsome couple and there was a long applause, indicating that everyone felt the couple had faced impossible challenges for the sake of their family and had come through.

The couple bowed in response, then once again from the gallery a string orchestra began to play a Strauss waltz. The defined rhythm was irresistible. John took Kate in his arms and they began to dance. The scene touched everyone and soon inspired the entire gathering to join them as they wheeled to the glorious melodies.

The happiness was infectious and a feeling of joy once more began to fill the air at the palace.

Fortunately the flight to Florida was not until midday and the Quartet were able to enjoy the function with the rest of the family. By tomorrow night the palace would be almost empty, just the staff and aunts Cecilia and Simonetta, who would supervise the big cleanup. For a couple of weeks the building had performed in the manner for which it was originally designed. It had witnessed the peaks of joy and desperate despair. It had seen three more of its offspring move on. The weddings that everyone had looked forward to were still a prospect for the future. No one could predict how long the investigation in Florida would take or when the Quartet would return to Florence.

The dancing was interrupted at 8 o'clock for a buffet dinner, something new. Previously important occasions were centered around beautifully dressed tables and many courses of delightful delicacies. Roberto's grand plan for the evening was a great success and reinforced his position as head of the family.

During the day Peter had finished adding all available information onto a floppy disc and together with the photographs of baby Sarah, everything was now prepared. As a foursome they would be able to cover a lot of ground very fast and they were very anxious to find the baby as soon as possible so as to unite the entire family.

It was well past midnight when everyone retired to bed, exhausted. The members of the orchestra had packed their instruments and left for another function in a different town. The kitchen staff were finalizing the clean up after an exquisite meal and the head butler made his final round, ensuring that all windows and doors were locked.

The air of the palace still contained a perfume of joy and laughter which the couples took with them to their individual rooms. The activities that continued there in private could only be imagined.

From the air of casual gaiety the previous evening, the morning had an almost military flavour for the four. They were awakened by the maid who brought them tea, following which, preparations for Florida controlled their activities. Each must consider their needs once they arrived there.

Throughout the morning guests with longer journeys were departing and wished to say their farewells to the four. Then it became their turn to leave for the airport. As they made their way to the waiting car those who still remained came to wish them God speed and finally they embarked upon yet another adventure. They had some indication of the opponent they were to face which gave them cause for concern, but there seemed to be a sort of aura around them that each one sensed, giving them confidence.

The weather continued miserable and cold, autumn days were imminent, autumn weather had already preceded them. The outer clothes they took to the airport with them they handed to the driver as they passed through the departure gate. Such attire would not be required in Florida.

The aircraft climbed out of Fiumicino and arrived in the thin air and blue skies above all the drizzle and cold. In the first-class compartment the flash of sunlight that flickered through the small windows as the aircraft banked out onto a westerly heading caused them to smile at one another.

"The seat-belt sign has been switched off." The voice of the stewardess invited them to relax for the long journey.

Nine

Even after a long, boring and tiring flight, Roberto, Valerie, Claudia and Peter were so intrigued by the beauty of the tropical plants in abundance at Orlando airport that, for half-an-hour before going into the city, they just wandered in and out of the small passageways between the towering bamboos, palms, bananas, and other exotic flora. The runways were far enough away that there was almost no ear-shattering noise or jet fuel odor to disturb the feeling that they could be in some tropical rain forest (one with concrete paths).

Everyone felt quite relaxed as they began the drive on the clean, wide boulevard to the hotel where they would stay just one night before initiating the search for baby Sarah.

The sun burned down, as a reminder that the temperature was 85°F in the shade. None had visited the subtropics before and having been accustomed to going from warm buildings to cold outside air, the opposite situation, from air-conditioned buildings and cars to very high air temperatures, seemed very strange.

The magnificent cabbage palms, at regular intervals along the streets and on landscaped areas in front of the buildings, were fascinating and frequently one of the party saw yet a bigger one and pointed it out to the others.

A quick stop at a beach-wear store on International Drive and ten minutes later they were mingling with the crowd, the only visual evidence of the fact that they were new arrivals in Florida being the now exposed white legs of Valerie and Peter.

The late afternoon and evening were spent resting and swimming in the hotel pool, followed by an early night, to compensate for jet lag.

The following morning was taken up with locating a house to rent. They found what they were looking for between Orlando and Kissimee, being reasonably central for access to the major cities in central and southern Florida where the five adoption agencies were scattered. They moved in immediately and began telephoning, posing as couples desperate to have a child. Appointments were made for the following day. Roberto and Valerie would travel west, while Claudia and Peter had to visit an agency in the south.

They had anticipated a slow beginning and with nothing else to do that day Roberto and Valerie spent the afternoon once more relaxing in and around the pool attached to the house, while Peter and Claudia went out to buy a lap-top computer and some electronic gadgets Peter thought might be useful once the group divided up.

The night was warm and as he lay in bed Roberto watched Valerie going through her preparations prior to joining him. For him it was still a novelty. She had been the first woman he had slept with since becoming sighted and every action she undertook, however mundane, gave him pleasure. He became very aroused as she finally approached the bed. Behind her the light was on and silhouetted her graceful curves through the very fine lace nightdress she wore.

"Stop just there," he requested, as she reached a point a couple of meters from where he lay.

She obeyed his request but asked, "Why?"

"I love to see you naked and yet I'm surprised to find it is even more sexually exciting to see you as you are at this moment. Please turn around slowly so that I may see every part of you, from all angles.

She turned slowly, as instructed, and as she arrived at a position facing him once more he threw back the bed cover and said,

"You see the effect it has on me?"

Now *she* stood for a few moments, running her eyes up and down *his* body. He habitually slept without pyjamas and the dark tan of his body and the thick black hair on his legs and broad chest contrasted with the bright white of the band-aid that covered the wound where the knife had entered on that terrible afternoon just before the train crash in Germany. Only a few inches away, in full and glorious presence, was the target she had aimed for. She shuddered at the thought, stepped forward and planted a gentle kiss on it as if to say, I am sorry for what I might have done.

The two years of dreams he had experienced before he even met Valerie flashed back to him but he realized they had been nothing compared with the reality he was now experiencing.

She was kneeling beside the bed, her auburn hair spilling over his stomach and chest. He ran his fingers through the hair he admired so much and she slowly planted kisses every inch as she moved toward his mouth. Then they finally kissed long and hard, both with their eyes fully open as always.

After a long and unhurried period of tender love-making, their sleep was deep and yet each had their brains and bodily functions triggered into full and immediate action by the violent sound of glass being shattered.

All four arrived almost simultaneously in the sitting room, the source of the disturbance, where each had the presence of mind not to switch on the lights. They froze for a moment, then the silence was broken by the sound of a motorbike accelerating away at high speed.

"I think we can switch on the lights now," Roberto suggested.

The main window to the sitting room was smashed and on the floor, amidst the broken glass, was the cause of the damage, a large stone wrapped in paper. Peter was nearest and removed the paper, then spread it out on the floor. There was a message, scrawled in large letters:

> You have spent enough time in Florida. Return
> home tomorrow alive, or in four coffins the next day.

The girls both looked very frightened and turned to their men for support, innocent gazes being met by confidence.

"We have been too relaxed. We thought we were in command of our situation; apparently we were not. At this moment we are the targets. They know who we are, where we are and probably our next moves. Tomorrow," Roberto paused from speaking while he checked his watch, "I should say today, that will all change."

Peter made the suggestion that the girls should return to Italy, a suggestion they refuted immediately.

"Look, they, whoever they are, obviously could have killed us at any time up to this moment. They did not and have granted us a further day's grace. Tomorrow is going to be a busy day for us and we need to be in good condition to face any potential problems." Roberto's words gave comfort. "Let's go back to bed and discuss what we will do in the morning. For the rest of tonight try to keep calm. We must assume the upper hand tomorrow. Good night, Peter, good night, Claudia, let's go, Valerie."

When selecting a house to rent the criteria had been comfort and location. The new priority became to disappear and relocate, ensuring that this time they were not followed. They had been clumsy.

The house backed onto a lake, providing a possible alternative exit route. However, the problem was that they had no idea who was watching them and how many were involved. Chances were it was Le Pen who was in control. On the map his alligator farm was situated approximately 150 miles to the north. It had been their intention to pay him a visit a little later. Under the circumstances perhaps a change of schedule was called for.

No one slept very well after the interruption of the night, feeling somehow very vulnerable. When morning came they had an early breakfast by the pool under a clear blue sky and the rising sun, which heralded a new Florida day.

"This is what I suggest," Roberto began. "We will drive to the airport, taking everything with us. There we will go through the motions of enquiring about flights back to Europe. We don't know how we are being monitored but there is a way we can reverse the situation while giving the impression we are returning to Europe. We haven't much time so let's get started and I will give you the rest of the details as we go along, if everyone is in agreement." He glanced around at the other three, each of whom replied in the affirmative.

On arrival at the airport they returned the rental car, then called the real estate agent and cancelled that agreement also. They were now mobile once more and felt a little less conspicuous. From the time they left the house they had all four kept a good lookout but had not seen any signs of being followed.

They sat in a small cafe in the airport where Roberto continued with his plan. They would split up. First the girls would go to the rest-room. While they were gone Peter would first move to a new position, then Roberto to another. Five minutes later the girls would exit the rest-room and move to yet a third agreed position, the thought being to confuse whoever may be watching them. The next step was for Roberto to contact the airport police who could in turn contact the Maresciallo in Florence. Once their credentials were established they would, hopefully, get some assistance from the local police.

Five minutes after they split up the girls left the rest-room, as agreed, and were met by police who escorted them into an office away from the public area, where Roberto was waiting. Then Peter received the same treatment.

The police were very cooperative and it was clear they had been given very good character reports by the Maresciallo.

Now they were out of view, Peter arranged to rent a light aircraft, which was shortly ready on the apron. The police transported them and their baggage to the Piper Twin Commanche and they climbed aboard, following which Peter took the seat of pilot-in-command and began to perform the preflight checks, which came as a surprise to the other three, none of whom knew he was a pilot.

"Well, you didn't ask."

Once they were clear of the airport zone Peter took the aircraft down to a low altitude and headed north-west until the coast-line of the Gulf of Mexico came into view. There he descended to an even lower level and turned north, following the beach.

"Look along the coast line about 50 miles north of Tampa," Peter instructed, as he handed them the map. "You will see a small town by the name of Crystal River. The airport there is our destination."

As a nuclear power station came into view, further up the coast, the aircraft climbed and turned east. Shortly after the airfield could be seen almost directly ahead and they were cleared to land. Peter made a perfect touchdown, confirming his ability as a pilot. The cockpit was very hot and they were glad to get into the small, air-conditioned airport building, where they had coffee and began to feel confident they had shaken off their pursuers.

"OK, no more houses. From now on we will stay in motels. By the way, I cancelled our appointments for tomorrow. We have to presume that Le Pen knew of our arrangements and would set traps for us; however, they can't remain there indefinitely. We will have to lie low for a couple of days. It's possible we've hit a nerve with one of the agencies we called. The call could have been traced and that was what brought about our problems. We must consider ourselves lucky we were given a day to leave. The day after tomorrow we will drive down to the alligator farm. They won't be expecting us to go on the offensive."

Claudia asked if she and Peter could make enquiries about the agencies while Roberto and Valerie went to the alligator farm. Roberto replied that he thought it best that they remain as a foursome from now on, no more splitting up. They must be prepared to move more slowly but be in constant contact.

During the next two days they visited the wildlife parks at Homosassa and Silver Springs, observing the alligators there and asking many questions about the prehistoric-looking beasts. They then hired a boat and did some fishing in the Gulf of Mexico where the water temperature was unbelievably warm. Swimming from the fishing boat was so pleasant no one was in a hurry for the day to end.

The drive down to where Le Pen had his farm was uneventful and with almost empty roads they were able to feel sure their presence was undetected. They arrived in the small town in the late evening and went directly to the police station.

The local police realized they intended to break into the house at the alligator farm and were turning a blind eye. They could not know officially, although they were equally curious to know what Le Pen was up to. For the time being all charges against Le Pen were conjecture. Nothing could be proven.

As far as they knew Le Pen was staying at the house, making it impossible to enter in the daytime. The police made layouts of the farm and floor plans of the house available, according to which the alligator pens were scattered all over the land and were even quite close to the house.

"There must be a terrible smell at the farm," the sheriff warned as he wished them good luck. They would have the advantage of two-way communication back to the police station in case of emergency.

It was after 11:30 p.m. when they began the five-mile walk to the farm. The decision to walk was reached to obviate the necessity of trying to hide a vehicle that would look conspicuous if it were seen parked anywhere nearby.

There was a half-moon, which gave them just sufficient light to follow the small country track that led to the farm. During the afternoon there had been a very heavy thunderstorm and the frogs were reciting poems in its honor and singing entire operas in praise of their liquid habitat.

Hopefully, snakes would be sleeping underground now, waiting for the next day's hot sun to match their blood temperature.

As they made their way along the path there came the sound of a vehicle approaching from the direction of the farm. They quickly hid themselves behind some oak trees that looked very tropical, hung with Spanish moss swinging in the light evening breeze.

A jeep passed them splashing mud that didn't reach the cab, mounted high above huge wheels and extended suspension struts. Once it was well out of sight Roberto took out a small flashlight and checked the list, provided by the police, of vehicles associated with the farm. The number corresponded to that of the truck registered to Le Pen. They had seen there were four men travelling in the truck and hoped that signified the house would be empty.

The sheriff had been right. As they drew close to the house the smell became almost overpowering and the awareness that they were now surrounded by large numbers of alligators, in the dark, even though the creatures were caged, caused them to proceed with great trepidation.

At the house there was one light in the hallway, suggesting there was no one home. They made their way to the back of the house and cut open a screen on a sun-room adjoining the house. The back door of the house was unlocked and they crept furtively in.

Peter suggested that one of the girls should wait outside with a two-way radio and warn them if the truck or any other vehicle was approaching.

"I'll go," Claudia offered. Valerie's arm had improved dramatically in just one week to the extent that she had already begun slipping off the now loose plaster cast and exercising as much as she could. Even so it was agreed that it would be better for Claudia to act as watchman. She went outside once more, feeling even more exposed, while the other three continued through to the room they hoped would contain any documents Le Pen retained at the house.

Sure enough, in the corner of the room stood a filing cabinet which fortunately was not locked. Roberto began to open the top drawer but as he did so all the lights in the house immediately switched on and an ear-shattering, raucous alarm began to sound. So unexpected, the sudden bright lights and ear-splitting noise triggered four hearts to break-neck speed.

"Damn," Roberto cursed, "he is no fool, this Le Pen."

Peter quickly ran outside, located the main power box and switched off the supply, causing the lights to go off but having no effect on the audible alarm which was causing them considerable distress. He then hurried back inside and found the alarm control box, mounted on a wall near the main entrance. With a screwdriver he removed the front cover, exposing a mass of wires, a sort of spaghetti junction to most, but to Peter it was just a question of locating the battery feed. In less than half a minute the noise stopped. The sudden contrast of absolute silence gave the effect of silence being a different type of noise, a very strange phenomenon.

Peter then went to find Claudia, who was terrified, unable to hear or speak on the two-way radio because of the noise level. He told her not to worry but to continue to keep a good look-out and her ears tuned, once her hearing returned.

Now that the alarm was deactivated, Roberto was able to search the files in peace, slowly working his way from the top drawer through the second and third, all of which related to the farm.

The bottom drawer contained more interesting data and one of the files was headed adoption. Roberto opened the file and quickly flicked through the papers until he found a letter from an adoption agency they had telephoned a few days before. A nerve *had* been touched.

Peter photographed all the pages with a miniature camera, then Roberto returned the papers to the filing cabinet and closed the drawer. They had found what they came for and felt very satisfied but they were still at Le Pen's farm. It was important to remain calm and in that state they slowly retraced their steps.

One hour later they were back at the police station, discussing with the sheriff what they had found, when there came a telephone call from Le Pen, complaining that his house had been broken into. The four had removed some relatively valuable items from the house with the intention of creating the impression that it had been a simple burglary.

"I will be there in ten minutes," the deputy assured the caller.

The sheriff, together with the four, remained at the police station while the deputy drove the short distance to the farm. He had never met Le Pen before and was shocked by the terrible burn scars on Le Pen's face, scars he had received when a bomb he was placing detonated unexpectedly.

"Listen, cop, I know who was here this evening and so do you. Where are they?"

"I don't know what you're talking about and suggest you don't take that threatening attitude with a police officer."

"I don't care who the hell you are. Look," Le Pen ripped the pistol from the deputy's holster and threw it into a corner. "Now you will do what I say. First you will tell me where they are, then you will return to your headquarters and put out an arrest warrant for them."

Le Pen certainly inspired fear, but on this occasion it was not enough. The young, inexperienced deputy had seen many films in which the police were always invincible. He took a deep breath and began to speak with renewed confidence, just as he had seen in the movies.

"I am going to take you downtown. You are under arrest for assaulting a police officer."

The deputy stepped forward, taking a pair of handcuffs from his belt, with the intention of hanging them around the wrists of Le Pen.

For a moment Le Pen laughed, then he took a firm hold on the deputy's throat with his strong hand, and smashed the back of his head hard against the wall behind. The deputy lost consciousness immediately, which was probably just as well for him, that is, until the next morning.

It was perhaps 8 a.m. when he awoke. Le Pen had extended his sleep with an injection. As he came out of his merciful sleep he looked around, realizing that he was outside the building. He began to move but as he did so it became obvious to him that he was not on the ground. Whatever he was on began to swing and soon he knew the answer. He was lying on a plank, approximately six feet by one foot, suspended above a small pond in which there were many alligators. Then his eyes met those of Le Pen.

"So, cop, you're awake. You have tried my patience so much I've decided you only have one minute to give me the answer and in case you've forgotten the question, where are they? Answer the question and you will be lowered and released. Keep quiet for one minute and you will never speak again."

"I don't know what you're talking about. I came to investigate a burglary."

Le Pen ignored the reply and began counting seconds as he looked at his watch. He arrived at 58, 59, and the deputy began to panic.

"I swear I don't know wh ..."

Le Pen's knife cut the rope holding the plank and there followed a mammoth splash, as both the plank and deputy crashed into the pond of alligators, then water being thrashed, then many terrifying screams, then silence.

"Idiot," Le Pen grunted as he went back into the house.

Once inside he took a pump shotgun down from the wall and began to load cartridges as he walked through to the room where the filing cabinet stood. Everything on the surface looked quite normal but he knew differently. He slid the bottom drawer open and just looked at the position of the files for a moment.

"So they know," he muttered to himself.

He began to walk out of the house just as his truck arrived, with three rough-looking characters on board. They glanced over at the pond where there was a lot of activity, the dirty brown water being churned up as the alligators fought for limbs. One remarked,

"So you had a visitor."

Le Pen ignored the comment. "The cops will be here soon. I want the three of you to take up positions along the roadway in front of the house, keep hidden and about ten yards apart. When they arrive blast them to hell. At the most there will be two squad cars. They must not have the opportunity to use the radio. The operation must be very rapid."

This was just the sort of job they enjoyed and the three grinned at one another as they set off to take up their positions. Once they had left, Le Pen went back inside the house and began to pack a bag, then returned to the room where the files were and selected a few which he stuffed into the bag also. He continued through to the garage, opened a safe in the floor and took from it a large briefcase, then threw it and the bag into the back of the jeep.

As Le Pen left the farm on a back road, he deliberately drove the jeep into the fences of the pens housing the alligators, smashing them down. The noise of the crashing fences disturbed the creatures and they began to make their way to the openings that now existed, then lumbered off in all directions.

There were just three more pens to attend to when he heard the sound of shotguns being fired in rapid succession. They are not very bright, he thought to himself, but that little task they will perform successfully. The gunfire ceased and le Pen completed the breaching of the last three fences. There were over 2,000 alligators at the farm in varying stages of growth, the biggest being twelve feet long. Oddly enough, that one would be quite simple to track down and put out of action. It was the 1700 babies, mainly just a few months old, that would create the real problem. They would scatter and create havoc for a long time to come.

What Le Pen didn't know was that, having not heard from the deputy for one hour, the sheriff anticipated a problem and called for reinforcements from the next town.

The first two squad cars had driven ahead and had been hit by Le Pen's three men but behind there were four other cruisers. They parked outside the farm entrance and began to close in on foot. Le Pen's men were busily occupied ripping everything they could from the squad cars and did not hear or expect more police to arrive on foot. Shortly the three were arrested and taken back to headquarters.

Roberto and Peter had decided, after consulting the map of the farm, to approach from the back and they were drawing close to the track leading to the back of the farm when Le Pen's jeep came swerving out. There was considerable damage to the front of the jeep and Roberto and Peter realized it was Le Pen. They made no effort to intercept him as he passed but relayed the information to the police.

Ten minutes later Le Pen was also under arrest. This time he would be put away for life for the murder of a police officer.

Once Le Pen's jeep was out of sight Roberto and Peter continued on up the track toward the farm and soon saw the damaged pens and large numbers of alligators loose. The jeep made considerable noise as it bumped along but not sufficient to muffle the scream that jolted them back to the moment. They had both been feeling very confident, patting themselves on the back with their latest success. Peter shifted gear and accelerated the rugged vehicle for all it was worth in the direction of the scream.

At their new speed and with the urgency of their mission of mercy, they could not avoid the many baby alligators that seemed to carpet the whole area. Many were crushed by the tires; others scattered with instinctive panic.

They arrived at a clearing and were confronted with the most horrific sight. A police officer was hanging onto the low branch of an oak tree with all his might, while an alligator had one of his legs in its mouth. The animal was about eight feet in length and intent on dragging its victim to the ground. One leg would provide a good meal but the whole body would be a feast.

Peter calmly edged the jeep to a point where the alligator was wedged against the tree; even so the animal retained its jaws in an iron grip on the police officer's leg. Peter turned off the ignition with the vehicle still in gear and engaged the handbrake. He then clambered over the bonnet of the jeep and rammed his hands into the mouth of the alligator. With all his might he pried and pried against the closing force of the alligator's mouth. Slowly, slowly he managed to ease open the great jaws, the animal released its grip on the police officer's leg and remained pinned against the tree.

Roberto in the meantime had also climbed onto the bonnet and between them they lowered the shuddering body into the jeep. The officer's leg was badly crushed and bleeding profusely and as he dropped onto the bonnet he lost consciousness.

Roberto and Peter lifted the limp body into the back of the jeep, then continued on until they joined the squad cars at the front of the house. The sheriff and his men were about to return to headquarters, being unable to even leave their vehicles because of the numbers of alligators.

As they began to drive in convoy away from the farm, several jeeps and trucks could be seen arriving from the opposite direction, carrying hunters hell-bent on containing the very dangerous animals, now moving in an ever-increasing distance from the farm.

Once they reached a safe distance the injured police officer was transferred to a squad car and rushed to the hospital. Peter and Roberto continued back to headquarters where Valerie and Claudia were waiting.

Ten

Police headquarters was besieged by radio, TV, and newspaper reporters, as the column of vehicles in which Roberto and Peter were travelling approached the building. Peter commented that the scene was similar to the confusion and squabbling of the baby alligators they had just left.

This was something they didn't need, so Peter pulled the jeep out of the column, parked where they were and called Valerie on the two-way radio.

"Valerie, listen, we think it best that you and Claudia get out of the building now, but avoid the correspondents. Just walk east away from the main entrance. We are in a black jeep, parked about 100 meters up the road."

Valerie and Claudia had been waiting in the operations room, listening to the various messages being passed between headquarters and the farm. They got up quietly, trying to look inconspicuous, and walked casually out of the front entrance, where, in reply to questions fired at them by the horde of reporters, they responded that they had nothing to do with the Henry le Pen inquiry, they had been picked up for a traffic violation. The reporters didn't want to waste time and accepted what they were told. A few minutes later, they joined Roberto and Peter in the jeep and were able to slip away.

While they were waiting Roberto and Peter had agreed not to worry the girls with all the gruesome details of what had happened at the alligator farm, just to keep it simple, and as they drove toward the motel they related the simplified version they had concocted. All four agreed they were very relieved Le Pen was now in custody.

It had been a long night and was now the middle of the morning. They hadn't slept at all, a condition that seemed to be repeating itself too often during the last week. Even so, sleep was at the bottom of the priority list for the moment. The adoption agency was located in Fort Lauderdale, some way from their current position at the motel. They planned to reach the city before nightfall, the best time to search for the answers they needed. Hopefully they would be able to locate records giving details of who had adopted baby Sarah and where she was.

Having agreed on their next move, they checked out of the motel, left the police jeep on the forecourt and climbed back into the rental car, then began their journey south.

It was another typical Florida morning, clear skies, no wind and beginning to heat up quite rapidly. They had just over 400 miles to travel and began a system of alternating drivers while the other three took naps. Once on the highway it was possible to maintain a good speed and after travelling for two hours they decided to stop for a meal at a restaurant by a lake.

They were becoming accustomed to the diverse fauna and flora of Florida and, being by a lake, there were plenty of examples to observe while they ate. The menu included 'Gatorburgers', which they declined, having seen enough alligators to last a lifetime. The subject of what they would eat prompted memories of a meal they had had in Vienna, three weeks before, when they had all agreed not to eat meat. Consequently they all chose 'Veggieburgers', which proved quite tasty.

Following their meal they set off once more, feeling less sleepy and thinking perhaps they were in the final stages of bringing the family back together.

On arrival at Fort Lauderdale they first checked into a motel near Route 95, then got hold of a map of the city from which they were able to find the road where the agency was located. It was about a twenty-minute drive from the motel. The time was nearly 5 p.m. and everyone decided to get some sleep, agreeing to meet up once more at 1 a.m.

Roberto had set the alarm, which disturbed both his and Valerie's deep sleep with its unpleasant and persistent beeping. Valerie called Peter and Claudia, who were also sleeping deeply.

Thirty minutes later they began driving to the road where the agency had its offices and as calculated reached the address twenty minutes later. The address was not a regular office building; instead it was a large mansion with three floors and extensive grounds. The night was illuminated by a full moon and the insect philharmonic was in full chorus.

"I have a bad feeling," Valerie cautioned. "I agreed to remain in the car and act as getaway driver in case of problems but now we are here I am not happy. Roberto, you said we would stay together as a foursome."

"Don't worry, we will be careful and you can be very useful waiting here in the car. Thanks to Peter, Claudia's bug will keep you informed as to what is going on. You will hear every move and every word. Just keep calm. We will be back in no time."

They could not park too close to the building, consequently Valerie was unable to observe the progress of the other three as they crossed the grounds at the back of the house. This time they didn't have the luxury of floor plans, consequently all they could do was to enter the house, by whatever means were possible, and search until they found the records they needed.

The doors were quite substantial and Peter was not very keen on the idea of breaking a window. The alternative was to scale the wall, using the down-pipe of the gutters, to a room on the first floor that had a window slightly ajar. Peter had no problem in reaching the window and he peered in to the dark room. Unfortunately the moon was on the wrong side of the building to be of any assistance. There was no alternative but to inch the window open, taking care not to make any noise, and climb into the room.

He was surprised at his own proficiency in an undertaking he had never performed before. Now he was inside, the amount of light from the moon, although not direct, was adequate to highlight the furniture and pick out the door, which appeared to be of a lighter colour than the rest of the room.

Soon Peter was downstairs opening the door where Roberto and Claudia were waiting. They went in and began their search of the rooms on the ground floor. The objective of the initial quick search was to locate a room furnished as an office. On the first floor there was none. They repeated the same procedure for the second floor and finally the top floor, where they found that three of the six bedrooms were occupied by a variety of people all of whom, fortunately, were sleeping.

Back on the ground floor Roberto suggested there might be a basement and sure enough, having checked many doors that gave access to closets, they tried a door that had a staircase behind. Once all three had passed through the door and it was closed, Roberto switched on the flashlight he was carrying. The staircase led down to an area that was decorated in a manner similar to the rest of the house, unlike a conventional basement.

They arrived at a door that had a powerful spring retaining it in the closed position and as soon as they entered they realized they had found the room they were looking for. Peter switched on the lights and as he did so a leather armchair swung around. There, sitting in the chair, was a heavily-built man in his forties. He blinked a few times to accustom himself to the light and said,

"Ladies and gentlemen, welcome. I have been expecting you. My name is David and I will be your host. Now, we know how you like to be together so we brought Valerie in to wait, while you were searching the top floor." He raised his voice and called, "Dennis, you can bring her in now."

A door opened and Valerie was led into the room. She walked across and joined the other three. So far there were no indications of force or intended violence so the three remained quiet, feeling rather in an inferior position for the time being.

David continued, "Please do sit. We want you to be comfortable for your last few hours. May I offer anyone a drink?"

The calm, confident words had a very frightening effect on the Quartet, all of whom declined the drink but accepted the offer of a seat. The armchairs had already been positioned in a group of four.

"You will, of course, be wondering how it was possible that I should be expecting you. The answer is quite simple. My very good friend Henry le Pen kept me aware of your moves until his arrest yesterday. He was, of course, not happy to have been taken into custody and attributes the entire blame to you four. I am in very great debt to Henry and when he asked me to revenge him for your acts I agreed without hesitation."

The business-like approach of David was beginning to get on Peter's nerves and he wanted to make a comment but decided to listen to the entire story first.

"Henry knew that you had found this address and I was confident you would come here straight from the farm. Well, here you are. Do you have any questions? I know how frustrated you must be and I want you to die peacefully."

"I don't have a question. I just want to remind you that there are four of us," Peter got it out this time.

"Come now, you surely don't believe there are only two of us. We have a great deal of experience and prefer to have the odds on our side."

Claudia was concerned for herself and her friends but still the first consideration was to find baby Sarah and she queried the situation.

"Baby Sarah, a very sweet little girl. The family were so pleased, even at $300,000 she was a bargain. Look at it this way. She will be brought up by a very rich couple in Miami. She will live a life of luxury and never have any problems. If she were old enough to make the choice, no doubt, she would readily accept such a lifestyle, compared with a father who will always be poor and a weak mother who is dying of cancer."

"What do you mean she's dying of cancer?" Valerie interrupted. "That's not true."

"Yes, my dear, I am afraid it is. When she was given her medical checkup before she began working for us, the physician discovered the first stages of ovarian cancer, though that did not make her less valuable to us."

"My God, you speak with the tone of an educated man," Roberto said with a tremor of anger in his voice, "but the words you use are those of a barbarian."

David, unmoved by Roberto's statement, continued,

"Business is the first consideration. If you begin thinking about people your progress is necessarily delayed. Now, as I told you I intend to carry out the wishes of my friend Henry; however, there is no need for you to suffer and therefore you will be pleased to hear that your deaths will be absolutely painless." What evil scheme had been devised they would presumably soon know.

"You may have noticed that this room has no windows and the only door that gives access to the floor above is substantial and seals tight under spring pressure. There is the first clue to your fate. You will be left alone here with a good meal and anything else I can give you that you would wish to have. This is not the first time we have carried out this operation and I am confident, from previous results, that you will simply drift into peaceful sleep. I think that is a very pleasant way to end the lives you have all four enjoyed to this point." As he spoke, David got up and beckoned Dennis to join him. The four made no comment or reply.

As their two captors left the room David turned and said, "Shortly you will be served a very fine meal. I sincerely hope you will enjoy it. We will not meet again, so I bid you farewell."

Again no one responded as the door closed firmly shut behind David and Dennis. Peter sparked off the conversation.

"It is obvious that this room is under very comprehensive surveillance and we must control our conversation accordingly. We are all frightened, but we must not give up hope. We are still alive, at the moment. I am going to whisper to each of you what is in our favour."

Peter began by whispering in Claudia's ear, then Valerie's and finally Roberto's. In each case the tension on their faces relaxed quite considerably after having heard his words.

Peter's scientific background included the study of poisonous gases. He was also an expert in audio and visual security, the ideal man to have around under the circumstances.

"David, I have a request. You did say you would try to meet our desires." Peter began to put his idea into action. "You can of course hear what I am saying. We are two couples who had intended to marry before becoming involved in this business. You have told us we are about to die; that being the case there is one last wish we would all four enjoy and that is to make love; however, you, as a gentleman, will appreciate that we would need to be in private for such an act. I am not suggesting that you provide another room, what I am asking is that you allow us to spend our last moments in a darkened room."

There was no response for a couple of minutes and they began to wonder if the message had been heard, then the clear voice of David could be heard over a loudspeaker at the end of the room.

"I will grant your request. In ten minutes you will be served the meal I promised. Thirty minutes later the lights will be turned off and you will be given one final hour to fulfill your desires."

"On behalf of my friends I would like to thank you," Peter responded.

There was a period of silence, then music began to play over the loudspeaker system. The music continued for a few minutes at a low level, then faded down as the door opened once more. Four silver trays were brought into the room and one handed to each. No one had any interest in eating and paid little attention to what was on the trays, though even at a glance it was evident the meals were *haute cuisine*.

"I see that you do not have any appetite. I am sorry," David's voice, once more over the loudspeaker system. "Perhaps you would care to skip directly to lights out?"

The four looked at one another and agreed

"Yes, we would like that," Roberto replied for everyone.

"I give you my word that you will now be left in peace for one hour, then a deep sleep will overcome you all, goodbye." With David's final word the lights faded down.

Peter knew that the gas pressure would be very low and he had already identified the two jets. Immediately the lights were out he cut two pieces of meat from his plate, tapped Roberto on the shoulder and whispered, "I need your help."

Carefully and quietly Peter led Roberto by the hand to the corner of one of the walls where he had seen a gas jet mounted. From the corner he measured the approximate distance he had estimated, then climbed on Roberto's back. The jet was quickly located and Peter rammed the piece of meat into the pipe.

They then went through the same procedure for the second jet and had just completed the operation when the music began to be played once more.

Peter then made his way to one of the loudspeakers and measured the cable attached to it from the wall, approximately three meters. Very good, there was a power socket at a distance of about two meters from the door.

Peter proceeded to disconnect the loudspeaker, then with the steak knife stripped half the length of each of the conductors. He then laid the two bare lengths of cable on the floor, just in front of the door. The other end he also stripped back a short distance and carefully pushed the wires into the power socket.

Once again, with the aid of Roberto's shoulders, Peter managed to reach the camera mounted high on the wall and proceeded to unscrew the lens to a point where the focus would create a completely blurred image.

The chances were when David returned he would be confident all four would be either dead or in a deep state of coma. Maybe he would have someone else with him but it was doubtful there would be more than two. They would have to take a chance on that.

Half-an-hour had passed since the lights were switched off. There was one other thing Peter wished to attend to.

He decided it would be reasonable for David to expect to find the bodies in some sort of disordered heap. That being the case if one body were missing and replaced by a simply constructed dummy he would probably not notice immediately.

Peter told Roberto to remove his sweater, jeans, and shoes, then, once again utilizing the steak knife, he cut open one of the large cushions from the four chairs and, with the aid of Valerie who had much more experience working in the dark, they stuffed the material from the cushion into the clothing. The result was a sort of dummy in the very approximate shape of a man,. How rough it was didn't really matter because the intention was that Roberto would be in a position behind the door when it opened. David would see what appeared to be four bodies on the floor, the one at the bottom of the heap being Roberto.

The hour was up. Peter had turned over the chair that was minus a cushion, then the four began to count down the remaining seconds, beads of perspiration forming on their foreheads. Would the meat plugs prevent any gas from entering the room?

They were in their positions as agreed. Roberto glanced at the luminous figures on his watch, five minutes past the designated hour. He had never killed anyone before and standing with a steak knife and fork in his hands he could not imagine that he would have the courage to complete that very final act. He was not the only one holding cutlery and having the same thought. They could not speak any more, just wait.

The minutes ticked by, each one protracted into the, seemingly, equivalent of an hour. There then came the sound of rushing air. The air in the room was being replaced to remove the deadly gas that supposedly filled the giant coffin. For maybe fifteen minutes the rushing sound continued, then there was silence once more.

Suddenly the room was lit up by the two spotlights mounted on the ceiling. Everyone remained absolutely still. Once more time dragged on into hours that were in fact a total of fifteen minutes, then the door opened.

"There is no gas indicated on the instrument." a voice confirmed.

Then the voice of David. "Fine, they are obviously all dead. Let's go back upstairs and finish preparing the containers. I wonder what the hell is wrong with that camera, must get it fixed tomorrow. Well, they certainly look very peaceful. Come on, we have a great deal to attend to."

Everyone waited a few minutes then Roberto got down on his knees and looked gingerly around the door, which was still open. The stairway was clear. He crept across to the heap of bodies and touched each one softly on the shoulder. They knew they must continue to work in silence and slowly raised themselves to the standing position, then one by one, with their shoes removed, and taking care to avoid the bare wires, began to file out into the short corridor leading to the staircase.

Under the stairs they found a small door, half normal size. Behind the door was a large space where various items of furniture lay strewn around. It was clear the furniture could not have been brought through the small door which Roberto continued to hold open. Peter gained everyone's attention and raised his finger in front of his lips indicating that they should continue to remain silent. He then climbed in through the small doorway and was followed by the other three.

The small room had yet another door, although it was at floor level, suggesting it was not an exit. Not only that but when Peter tried to open it he found it to be locked. In a final visual sweep of desperation the four surveyed the large area, all walls and ceilings. Approximately ten feet above them, they saw what was evidently an entrance from the garden that would probably be locked from outside. Even so it was worth a try.

Some of the pieces of old furniture were very heavy and to move them without making any noise presented a formidable task. However, finally they succeeded in arriving at a height where Peter, who was the most athletic, was able to reach the doors. Much to his surprise he succeeded in opening them. As he did so, there was a scream as someone entered the other room and stepped onto the bare wires. Peter quickly descended and hurriedly told everyone to hide behind the pile of furniture they had assembled.

Suddenly they heard cursing and the sound of running footsteps up and down the stairs, then a head peered through the small door and shone a flashlight on the pile of old furniture, following it up to the open trap door at the top. "Shit!" David's voice uttered a word he probably used very infrequently, "So they got away."

Once more the sound of footsteps on the stairs, then silence.

"Let's go," Roberto suggested. The four filed out through the small door, along the small passageway, up the stairs and out of the house. They were disappointed to leave with empty hands but at least they were still alive.

They could not return to the car Valerie had been taken from earlier, so once clear of the grounds they began walking in the direction of the shops they had seen on their way the evening before.

Their backs felt very exposed, expecting at any moment to be shot. However, this time they were fortunate and were able to reach the shopping plaza without seeing anyone. Once there they called the car rental company and informed them the car had been stolen. Then a taxi was called to take them back to the motel.

Eleven

The sheriff was not at all happy when Roberto called to give him details of the previous night's events.

"Thanks to your trying to play detective we may now have lost any possibility of finding the child. You withheld information that could have resulted in the apprehension of dangerous criminals. It's clear that David and the others will disappear and either take all the information with them or destroy it." The sheriff went on to instruct them to report to police headquarters in Fort Lauderdale and not take any further action relating to the matter.

They were certainly not going to report to the police. The situation was even more urgent now. If the police were able to find baby Sarah that would be fine but the Quartet would definitely continue with their own inquiries.

Everyone was very dejected following Roberto's conversation with the sheriff. They had expected sympathy. During the night they had come very close to death and had lost the one good lead they had, added to which, once again they were desperate for sleep, though before they could lay their heads down they would need to move once more. The difficulties were accumulating.

"I am going out to buy some form of transport," Peter said, in an endeavor to raise everyone's spirits. "We can't rent, the car would be traced too easily."

"OK," Roberto agreed. "But we need to move quickly. The police will surely be here very soon."

"Look," Claudia whispered and indicated where Valerie sat in the chair. She had drifted off to sleep.

Roberto took a cover from the bed and covered her. As he did so he kissed her gently on the forehead.

"The little birds, they are beautiful," Valerie was evidently having the same dream once more, "but why is the baby crying?"

"Where are the birds?" Roberto tried to prompt her to continue.

"In a white cage. It is very big and delicately shaped. "Sarah, don't cry. There, now, she's sleeping again."

Peter returned after only twenty minutes.

"Listen, we are only a few minutes' walk from a Greyhound bus depot. Don't you think it would be better to take the bus out of here?"

"Good idea," Roberto agreed, as he gently woke Valerie. "Grab a bag each and let's go."

"Where are we going?" Valerie had missed the discussion while she slept.

"You remember," Roberto replied with new enthusiasm. "David spoke of baby Sarah being with a wealthy family in Miami. That will be our next stop and we have more information. While you slept just now you were talking of coloured birds in a big white cage and of hearing a baby crying. We will visit pet shops and try to find someone who has such a cage." As they continued their discussion they began to walk toward the bus station.

"And?" Valerie queried.

"And what?" Roberto replied.

"Didn't I say any more?"

"No. Why, was there more?"

"When I heard the baby crying, I turned in the direction of the sound and saw a magnificent, apricot-coloured house by a river and there were some very strange trees. I have never seen trees, even similar, before. Maybe they were a figment of my imagination. They seemed to be like a group of tall thin trees that had been joined together, their trunks twisted and becoming wide just above ground level."

Fortunately there was not a long wait for the bus and less than an hour later they were in Miami.

On arrival they felt it would be quite safe to rent a car and soon were heading south, having tried all other points of the compass, each of which were uncomfortable to Valerie. South felt right.

By now the high rise blocks of Metro Dade were way behind and the car was edging along with the late afternoon traffic on Route 1.

"Red is important for some reason," Valerie posed an enigma. "I don't know why I have that notion. What could it mean?"

"How about Red Road?" Claudia suggested.

"I don't know. Why?"

"We have just passed Red Road."

"Try it," Valerie responded.

Peter, who was driving, pulled to the center lane and continued to the next traffic light. There he made a 'U' turn and as they approached the intersection of Red Road, he asked Valerie which way they should turn.

"I don't know, but let's turn right, as we are on this side of the road."

Peter did as instructed, then Roberto posed a question.

"Did we all see the sign?"

"Which?" was the unanimous reply.

"Parrot Jungle. As we turned I saw a sign indicating Parrot Jungle on this road."

"That sounds promising. Let's go there," Valerie said excitedly.

It was only a short journey to Parrot Jungle but unfortunately when they arrived the gates were just closing for the day. Scrutinizing the information relating to the park revealed that on display was a great variety of birds and tropical plants. It was agreed they would return the following morning.

Back in the car they continued in the same direction on Red Road and at the next junction turned left, back toward Miami. Shortly they began to pass expensive looking mansions and close to the edge of the road at regular intervals, many of the trees Valerie had described seeing in her dream.

"Let's have a luxury night at a beach hotel," Roberto suggested. No one argued with that idea and soon they were crossing the MacArthur Causeway, heading for Miami Beach.

All four were enthusiastic about the view and were paying little attention to speed limits until a police motorcycle appeared in Peter's mirror, blue lights flashing and obviously coming directly for them.

Peter pulled over and waited with the ignition turned off.

In his mirror he saw the police officer park his motorcycle and walk slowly toward their car.

"Good afternoon, officer," Peter's innocent greeting.

"Good afternoon, sir. You appear to be in a great hurry, I clocked you at 58 miles an hour."

"I have no excuse. No, we are not in a hurry and the only defense I can offer is that I was carried away with the beauty of the view and momentarily my attention was distracted, when I should have been observing the speed limit."

"So you are English. Let's see your driving licence, auto registration, and insurance."

Peter handed over his international driving licence and the car rental papers. The officer studied the papers for a few minutes, then asked to see the passports of the other three, which they passed him.

Armed with all their passports the officer went back to his motorcycle and apparently made a call on his radio.

"That's unfortunate," Roberto said. "We are so close to solving the mystery of baby Sarah and now it's probably over. Once he checks for information on us, presumably there will already be arrest warrants on file."

"You may imagine how I feel," Peter replied apologetically. "It was very stupid of me. I should have kept my eyes on the road. I can't believe I didn't see him."

"Don't worry," Roberto continued. "If I had been driving the situation would have been the same. The problem was the sharp contrast from being frightened last night to suddenly feeling free and happy."

"Well, now we will know, he's coming," Peter observed. Claudia took his hand and squeezed it gently, trying to give him confidence once more.

"OK sir, I am not going to give you a ticket this time but if I come across you doing one mile in excess of the speed limit again I will book you." He handed back their passports and as he did so Peter noticed his name tag, Joe Cellini.

"I see you have an Italian name. If I say *millegrazie* I am sure you will understand."

"That's correct. My family are from Liguria but I was born here. I noticed two of your passports are Italian. Are you on holiday?"

"Yes, we're touring southern Florida."

"Well, be careful in the city. You would be advised to keep to the hotel overnight."

"Thank you, you have been very kind and I will keep to the limit in future."

"Good luck."

Peter edged away very carefully and for a mile or so his eyes flashed between the odometer and the road every few seconds as four hearts settled down to normal beat.

The two adjacent rooms were on the tenth floor of the hotel building and gave magnificent views of the ocean, together with a considerable length of the coastline. Following a very fine fish dinner, cooked in a traditional Jamaican style, the couples retired to their individual rooms.

Peter and Claudia jumped into the hot tub, straight away, and explored each other while enjoying the thousands of bubbles massaging them as they rushed to the surface. Then Claudia suddenly became silent and sad. Tears began to run down her face and she put her arms around Peter's neck, searching for tenderness. Peter was baffled for a moment, then realized, as he looked once more at the surface of the water.

The bubbles. It was bubbles that had signified the end of the lives of both Eleanora and Gina. He held her close and marvelled at her jet black hair, glistening wet. Then he kissed her over and over again, ever more intensely, until her crying stopped and her mind became fully occupied with her love for him. Each became hungry for the other and their deep desires for the ultimate sensation of love were satisfied, finally acting as a sleeping potion.

As Roberto finished preparing himself for bed, Valerie was exercising her arm once more. Soon he was exercising his eyes, feasting on her beauty. She lay on the bed naked, with her long, slim legs very slightly apart. He knew how tired she was and was also anticipating deep relaxing sleep, even so he was roused at such a beautiful sight. He removed his pyjama trousers and moved closer to the bed. There he knelt and began to run his fingers softly all over her body, neglecting not a single centimeter.

Maybe he was too tender because soon her eyes closed and she drifted off to a land where love and life are true and free. For a few moments more Roberto continued to revel in the perfect woman who lay before him, then, realizing that his eyelids were also becoming heavy, he climbed on to the bed beside his sleeping beauty, kissed her once more and satisfied himself with the thought that his desires would be fulfilled another day. Shortly he joined her in that marvelous place.

At 8 the following morning the telephone on Roberto's bedside table began to ring. He had been resting with his eyes open for the previous thirty minutes, his mind reliving the short life he had had with Valerie. There had been no life before, she was so important to him. He picked up the receiver, confident he knew who was calling.

"Good morning. Are you both well and rested?" Peter's happy voice enquired.

"We are in good spirits and looking forward to chatting with the parrots," Roberto responded. "See you for breakfast in thirty minutes. OK?"

"Fine."

Valerie and Claudia were already half-way through their preparations, which was just as well. They both took a great deal of care over their appearances and half-an-hour would have been totally inadequate.

It was nearer forty-five minutes when Peter knocked on Roberto's door. All four were ready, looking very fit and happy. They greeted one another and took the lift to the ground floor.

Following breakfast they quickly got back into their routine again. Peter had a video, as well as a 35 mm camera prepared for any eventuality. He sat beside Roberto who began the drive to Parrot Jungle. Claudia and Valerie, in the back seat, were discussing the ridiculous clothes a German tourist had been wearing at the hotel.

It was only a thirty-minute drive to Parrot Jungle and soon they were wandering around the park, where they found the incredible variety of birds and tropical plants fascinating. Macaws flew freely and they came upon a reminder of Henry le Pen, alligators in various sizes lay like old knurled logs, immobile in the mud.

"They don't look so vicious," Valerie remarked, noticing that the monstrous, black beasts seemed not at all interested in moving.

Peter and Roberto looked at one another and grinned when they mentally recalled the hundreds of alligators at the farm running in all directions and looking extremely agile.

"No," Peter replied. "I suppose they only begin to move when they're provoked or when they're hungry."

"Look over there, "Claudia pointed, indicating a very large aviary, full of hundreds of birds busily discussing everything under the beautiful, hot sun. "Could that be it?"

Valerie stopped for a moment but decided that it was not the cage she had seen.

Peter began filming with the video camera; the wild life, plants and his friends. As he captured them on tape he thought to himself that, even with all the sadness and danger of the last three weeks, he was very happy, more than he had ever experienced before. It was obvious to him that tne major contributing factor to his present state of mind was the joy of having such good friends.

He began to pan the camera beyond where they stood when, in the view-finder, he caught sight of a young couple walking with a pram. He attracted the attention of the other three and they agreed to move closer to try to catch a glimpse of the baby.

It was not 100 percent sure because, for the Quartet, all babies looked alike; however, in another aviary, near where they now stood, something disturbed the birds and suddenly there was a cacophony of thousands of small birds chirping and flying in confusion all around the beautiful sculptured, white cage. As they gradually quieted down any doubts the Quartet had about the baby were dismissed because the sudden noise had caused the baby to cry. Valerie in particular felt very confident that the baby was in fact Sarah. Peter continued to film and succeeded in getting a good shot of the baby.

Roberto took the 35 mm camera from Peter and began snapping in all directions. One blink of the shutter opened and closed with an image of the baby clearly fixed on the film.

Gradually the Quartet moved further away and for the next two hours kept an eye on the family from some distance away, not wishing to attract attention to themselves. Even when the couple with baby Sarah left the park, Claudia simply wrote the registration number of their car, which turned out to be a white Rolls Royce. They remained behind.

At the nearest post office, Roberto sent a fax to John and Kate with the good news. Now they had definitely located baby Sarah it was just a question of waiting for her parents to arrive from Italy. They were going to set out almost immediately and expected to arrive in Miami within twenty-four hours by whichever route was the quickest.

After much discussion the Quartet agreed that for the moment they would not make contact with the police. The family that had adopted Sarah were evidently very rich and if things became complicated it might be necessary to kidnap the child. Certainly John and Kate would want to have her the moment they arrived. Red tape could drag the process on for days, which would be bad for John, Kate, and Sarah.

There was time to kill now and from the various possibilities available to them it was agreed they would visit the Vizcaya museum in south Miami, a villa built in the Italian renaissance style.

They had a Chinese vegetarian lunch, then drove to the museum where they spent the afternoon. Roberto remarked that the air conditioning at the museum was a great advantage over *Il Palazzo*. Otherwise, although the building was an interesting endeavor to create some imitation history, the only genuine article was a Roman altar from the 1st century AD.

The film was ready at 5 p.m. and Roberto faxed a copy of the photograph of the baby back to Florence, just to be absolutely sure.

As they drove back to the hotel the Quartet wondered how they would adapt to normal life after their adventures of the past three weeks; nevertheless, they were all anxious to return to Florence, marry and move into the gate houses.

Peter had been keeping a secret from everyone. When Claudia gave up modelling and he resigned his post with the electronics company, he spoke of an invention he had been working on for years and said he would explain the details after their honeymoons. Since there had been a delay in the wedding date, the other three were very curious to hear what it was Peter had invented. He would not budge. They tried everything they could think of to try and make him tell them. Claudia even tickled him, coming very close to a confession, because he was extremely sensitive. But in the end they respected his wish to keep it a secret.

There was a message at the hotel from Cecilia. She had seen the photograph Roberto faxed and compared it with the original, she was also confident that the photographs were of the same baby. The message went on to say that the flight carrying John and Kate would arrive in Miami at 3 p.m. the next day.

Roberto's call to the ambassador in Bucharest was received with great enthusiasm and the Quartet gained a lot of satisfaction knowing that they had been instrumental in resolving such a difficult problem. It was just a matter of a day or so now, then everything would be finalized.

Roberto gained everyone's attention and said, "I have something important to tell you all." He stepped across to where Claudia stood, took her hand and announced, "Today is the birthday of my dear sister." Following his happy statement Roberto kissed her on both cheeks. His embraces were followed by Valerie giving her a one-arm hug, then Peter, who exaggerated somewhat, not having any qualms about kissing her passionately before his friends.

"We must celebrate," Peter recommended as he recovered his breath from the long kiss.

"Let's see," Roberto said, thinking out loud. "How about a candle-lit supper on a boat? It's a beautiful evening."

"I would enjoy that very much," Claudia said excitedly.

Roberto called reception and asked for information regarding their wish. He was given one or two suggestions and they called and confirmed a table for four on a ship that was moored in the harbour.

They had one-and-a-half hours, just sufficient time to find new evening gowns for the girls and dinner jackets for Roberto and Peter.

They had no difficulty in locating a store offering elegant attire and with their regular clothes in bags they left the store looking very splendid.

The entire evening passed with great joy and while they enjoyed an excellent dinner a small band played quietly. Roberto excused himself for a couple of minutes and shortly after he returned to the table the musicians began to play a song Claudia had loved as a girl. She thanked Roberto for thinking of it and remembering but shared the sentiment of the words with Peter.

The day ended on a very pleasant note.

Twelve

There was one other important task to perform before going to the airport to meet the flight from Italy. They needed to have the name and address of the adoptive parents of baby Sarah.

Taking with him the number of the white Rolls, Peter went to the tag office and was surprised how simple it was to get the information. In England it would not be possible.

Now they knew the names, Karl and Erica Schwartz, and address, Valerie was very curious to know whether the house was in fact painted apricot colour, as in her dream. To satisfy her curiosity they drove along the road where the house was situated and sure enough as they passed by the colour was confirmed to be apricot, not only that but the style of construction was also as she had pictured, a fact that gave her goose bumps.

It was nearly lunch time and the general consensus was for pizza. They had passed an interesting looking restaurant the evening before, sporting the Italian flag and boasting genuine pizza. Peter thought he remembered where it was and set off in that direction. As they drove Roberto began to add a note of caution to their situation.

"From the time we began to look for the family of the ambassador we have had a couple of difficult situations but, all things considered, we have been very fortunate; both in getting clues, thanks to Valerie, and extricating ourselves from potentially dangerous situations, thanks to Peter. I think we should remember, however, that it isn't over yet. No doubt David, for one, would be very happy to take his revenge on us. I don't want to frighten you all but we have been relaxing and feeling very pleased with ourselves. We must remember that we are a thorn in the side of a powerful organization."

"That's right," Peter agreed. "Perhaps we should take evasive action now, before it's even needed."

"What do you mean?" Valerie asked.

"The hotel, for example. We have been there for three days now. It's a very conspicuous location and we have been coming and going, occasionally dressed to kill, actually drawing attention to ourselves."

"Well, I'm glad we're discussing the matter now, before something serious happens," Roberto continued. "Let's go back to the hotel, settle the account and move out immediately. We should change the rental car, too."

It was agreed and one hour later they had checked out of the very comfortable beach hotel and changed the car for a van. There was just over one hour to wait before the flight was due to arrive.

No more flashy clothes. Everyone had changed to shorts and simple shirts with the intention of blending with the crowd. Even Peter and Valerie's legs had begun to colour with regular exposure to the sun. They didn't look quite so English any more.

At Miami International Airport the flight arrived on time, which was a great relief to all. John and Kate were very excited as they came through the arrival gate. They hadn't dreamed that in such a short time Sarah would be found. The atmosphere was very happy and friendly with much cuddling and thanking.

Claudia looked deep into Kate's face and wondered whether she knew she had cancer. Whatever, for the moment her ecstatic joy should not be spoilt by such talk, but in Kate's interest, Claudia thought to herself, she must bring up the subject in a couple of days. She should be receiving treatment and Claudia had a very good friend who was a leading specialist in the field.

John and Kate had the good sense to travel light and the van had no problem in accommodating six people, with their luggage, as they began to drive away from the airport.

Roberto, who, by general agreement, continued to make the ultimate decisions, decided they would drive to the southern outskirts of the city and find a modest motel, thereby maintaining a low profile and being within a reasonable distance of the apricot house.

The motel they checked into was decidedly a contrast to the hotel where they had spent the previous three nights. Maybe it was the location that instilled a sense of impending problems, although not even Valerie could say why they felt so.

John and Kate had left Florence before the fax of the photograph of Sarah had arrived. Once they saw the original their excitement grew and they began to agitate to go to the house immediately.

"Listen," Roberto said with a very serious note. "The young couple who have Sarah paid $300,000 for her and even though they have only had her a couple of weeks, you can be sure they would have no intention of just handing her over, even if they knew the true story."

"Well, surely the law would be on our side," Kate's voice had a slight quiver to it. "We have brought as much information as we could lay our hands on, birth certificate, etc. and my father-in-law will be able to sort out any international problems."

"Of course," Roberto continued. "What I am afraid of is a protracted court case, which you would certainly win, but sometimes in the U.S.A. these things can drag on for years. My concern is to have Sarah back in Europe with you at the earliest possible time."

"Forgive me," Kate apologized. "You know we have had a very difficult time for the past three weeks and are nervous and impulsive. I am happy to leave everything to you."

"Wait a moment," John interrupted. "We are talking about our child. She was kidnapped, sold and adopted illegally. Just tell me where the house is. I will go in and take her."

"Sorry, John, in your's and Kate's interest I am not prepared to do that. Just hear me out. You will have your baby much more quickly if we do things sensibly."

Kate began to cry. She was on the point of breakdown and Valerie put her arm around her to comfort her.

"Don't worry, Kate, everything will be all right but just remember that money talks in America. We have made inquiries about the family and they are worth over a billion dollars. They can twist the law with their spare change."

"It's not that. I believe in you, you have done so much for us and I am confident you know the best way to get our baby back. It's John I am upset about, I ..."

"Oh, Kate, I'm sorry, you are right. I don't know what would have happened to us without you four. I didn't mean to suggest that I wanted to jump in and take over. I am also happy to leave it up to you."

"OK," Roberto began once more. "Do you have Sarah on one of your passports?"

"Yes, she's on mine," Kate replied, drying her eyes. "It was necessary when we took her to Italy."

"Fine. Then tonight, we will go in and get Sarah out." Big words, Roberto thought to himself as he uttered them. Peter, Valerie, and Claudia were also taken by surprise by Roberto's confident statement.

John and Kate, on the other hand, became very enthusiastic and had visions of flying back to England the next day, a complete family once more.

There was silence for a moment, then Roberto continued.

"We are going to place ourselves in serious jeopardy with the law and will need a minimum of twelve hours from the time we have Sarah, before the alarm is sounded."

"What do you propose?" Peter asked.

"The first problem is, we don't know how many people are in the house. However many there are we are going to have to put them all out of action for twelve hours and kidnap your own child. It sounds ridiculous, I know."

"There could be a power failure," Peter suggested. "They would call the power company, but the telephone would be connected to us, which they would not know, of course. We need a small van, similar to those used by the power company."

"I like it." Roberto breathed a sigh of relief. He had been saved from a rash promise. "Tell us more."

"I am just thinking out loud for the moment. I have electronic meters, tools etc. It's no problem looking the part, but how about ID? Let's see. I know, I can design a card on the lap-top, get it printed out on a laser printer and slip it into a plastic holder."

"Fine, and I will be your assistant," Roberto proposed.

"Well, I don't think so. I will call you from the house on my car radio and you will come with the van. That will give me some delay while I assess the number of people in the house. The rest we will have to contrive as we go along."

"That seems reasonable to me," Roberto said with admiration for Peter's ability to improvise. "Sometimes, if planning is too complicated and perfect, the plan relies on things happening that don't happen, and then confusion reigns."

"Where do I come in?" John questioned.

"You will arrive with Roberto and assist with deactivating whoever is in the house. The final phase will be the arrival of the girls to collect the baby, though they can also be in the back of the van."

The plan began to take shape as they discussed the potential problems and listed everything they would need. It was, by then, 6 p.m. and everyone was detailed to find and obtain the items on the list. By 8 p.m. they were once more assembled and ready to begin.

Their first good fortune was that the almost full moon was covered by clouds and even though the sun had only sunk half-an-hour previously, it was already quite dark. The road with the apricot-coloured house was quiet, with almost no traffic, so they just took a chance. Peter was dropped, with a small dog they had obtained, approximately 50 meters down the road. He began to walk in the direction of the house, doing his best to look nonchalant, just taking his dog for an evening stroll.

The house was set back from the road and had a large landscaped area by the entrance gates, with bushes and several of Valerie's trees. The telephone access point was a box underneath one of the bushes and Peter carried out his modifications within a matter of seconds. Then with a tree pruner he carefully cut the neutral cable feeding power to the house, the lights went out instantly and sure enough thirty seconds later the telephone rang in the van.

"Hello, this is the power company. My name is Kimberley. How may I help you?" Valerie made her best effort at an American accent, not that the caller cared or noticed. The important thing was to have power restored as soon as possible. "We will have an engineer there within ten minutes."

"Thank you."

The voice was that of a young woman and in the van they began to speculate as to whether or not it had been Erica, the adoptive mother.

Peter returned shortly after.

"Here, take this stupid dog. He peed on my leg while I was cutting the cable. Lucky for him I didn't accidently cut the live feed, he could have had a very delicate shock." Everyone laughed rather more than was justified. Their nerves were at a high pitch, resulting in the exaggerated laughter.

Peter climbed in, they drove off to where the white truck was parked and ten minutes later Peter was once more at the gates of the apricot house, sounding the horn of his truck. The gate phone was out of action, with no power, and it took the occupants of the house a few minutes to realize, but soon the figure of a man was seen approaching the gates.

"Hi."

"Hi, I'm from the power company. What happened?"

"I don't know. The lights suddenly went out. Let me see your ID."

Peter took out the card he had prepared and handed it to the man, who squinted at it in the light of a weak flashlight he was carrying, then handed the card back to Peter and opened the gates.

"You go on up to the house. My wife is there she will let you in. I am going to close the gates."

Peter did as instructed. The man was definitely Karl, the one they had seen at the Parrot Jungle. That meant he was about to meet Erica, the adoptive mother. He pulled up in front of the house, which was magnificent. Even without light it was evident it must have cost millions.

Erica was waiting at the top of the steps with a hurricane lamp and asked where Peter wanted to begin.

"The fuse breaker box."

"It's in the basement. You had better come in. Oh, dear, the baby is crying. Will you come quickly, please."

Peter skipped up the steps and in a moment was following Erica inside.

"There's the door to the basement. Can you find your own way now?"

"Sure, you go ahead."

Peter opened the door and went through. He then switched off his flashlight and looked back around the door. The silhouetted figure of Erica was hurriedly climbing the stairs and from the amount of time the light was still visible after she reached the top, Peter estimated she had gone into the first room on the right, at the head of the stairs. He could hear the baby crying also.

Peter made his way downstairs, opened the main fuse box and connected his meter with a couple of crocodile clips to two of the wires, at which moment Karl appeared and asked the situation.

"Nothing, so far. Just give me a few minutes."

Peter continued to appear to be controlling the fuse box connections, as Karl drew closer. When he was immediately alongside Peter turned, grabbed him and forced a thick cotton-wool pad, impregnated with chloroform, against his mouth and nose. Karl struggled for a moment but he was no match for Peter and soon his legs gave way and he succumbed to the anesthetic.

From his tool box, Peter took a large band-aid and applied it to Karl's mouth, then tied his wrists and ankles in such a way that he would be totally immobilized if he recovered consciousness before it was intended.

Having successfully completed that stage of the operation, Peter decided to proceed upstairs. He assumed there was no one else in the house. If there had been he would have expected them to appear when he arrived on the scene.

"Excuse me, madam, may I come up?" Peter stood at the foot of the stairs awaiting a reply.

Erica opened the first door on the right at the head of the stairs, as he had expected, and told him that he might. Peter climbed the stairs and when he arrived at the top told the woman he needed to check some circuits in the upstairs rooms. She accepted that everything was in order and waited as he apparently was about to pass her. In a matter of seconds she was also anesthetized, gagged, and tied.

Peter continued along the landing to the second door. It led to a bedroom, probably that of Karl and Erica. The ideal place to accommodate them, he thought.

Outside in the van the rest of the group were becoming rather concerned at having heard nothing. However, they had no alternative but to continue to wait for Peter to call on the two-way radio.

Fifteen minutes after Peter had driven away, they saw the white truck returning.

"Look, Peter is coming back. Maybe he has a problem," Claudia said with a worried note in her voice.

The van drew up alongside the vehicle the rest of the group were in and Peter climbed out. He then went to the passenger side of the vehicle and opened the door. There was not enough light to see what he was carrying until he was immediately alongside them.

Much to everyone's surprise when they opened the door to give Peter access, he thrust a carry-cot in onto an empty seat. In the carry-cot was baby Sarah sleeping peacefully. He then jumped in himself.

"Let's go."

Roberto was sitting in the driver's seat and wasted no time waiting for explanations. He started the engine, slipped into drive and pulled away smoothly and quietly.

Everyone was bursting with excitement and questions but succeeded in suppressing their curiosity for the sake of the sleeping baby. They decided to not even switch on the interior light and John and Kate, who were aching to take Sarah in their arms, had to just restrain themselves.

After Peter's experience on the journey to Miami Beach, Roberto maintained a speed within the limit. It would not be a good time to meet Officer Cellini again.

There was a possibility of arriving in time for the 11 p.m. flight. Peter had conducted the operation very quickly and it was only 9:15 when they began the short journey to Miami International Airport. Roberto called American Airlines and discovered that seats were available on the midnight flight, arriving in Nassau at 1:05 a.m. He confirmed that they would pick up the tickets at about 10 p.m.

"We will need some baby food and diapers," Kate suddenly remembered.

"That's right," Roberto replied. "I will stop at the next store that's still open."

It was amazing that Sarah slept so peacefully, with such dramatic events taking place around her. Maybe some instinct calmed her now that she was once more with her natural mother.

"Once we arrive at the airport," Peter suggested, "instead of leaving the van in the car park there, now that we have time, I could drive it to the Greyhound bus station and get a taxi back here. Create a little more confusion for the police."

"Good idea." Roberto agreed. "Look, there's a store open." He parked the van and the three girls went in to select what was necessary for the baby, each imagining themselves as mothers.

The final leg of the journey to the airport was soon completed and Peter left to take the van. He would park it at the bus station in a prominent position to attract attention. For the benefit of whoever found it they left on the back seat a special deposit made by Sarah in a diaper. There would be no doubt then, and enquiries would be concentrated on busses out of Miami.

By the time Peter returned to the airport, there was still forty-five minutes before the flight was due to depart for Nassau. Sarah had awakened and Kate and John were in seventh heaven playing with her and kissing her, inhaling that sweet milky, baby perfume that makes them so attractive during the first year or so. They found an area with very few people and Peter took the opportunity to satisfy everyone's curiosity as to how he had been able to come out with Sarah alone.

Once Karl and Erica were sleeping, Peter had transferred them to their regular bedroom and lifted them on to the bed, both secured so that they would be unable to move without assistance, which would arrive in the morning. Peter reset a clock on the mantelpiece to 5 a.m., then smashed it in the hope of confusing the police as to the time of the incident.

Peter found the baby sleeping peacefully and simply transferred her carefully into a carry-cot that was in the nursery. From that point on they knew the story.

Everything had gone off without a hitch and apart from a few cars passing by there had been no sign of pedestrian traffic, probably because it was such a dark night.

Everyone was very impressed with what Peter had achieved single-handedly and Roberto was puzzled as to how Peter was able to buy chloroform.

"I didn't. I bought bleaching powder, acetone and sulfuric acid and made my own. I apologize for keeping it a secret from you all but I had decided previously that if the couple were alone in the house, I could probably handle it myself. Consequently, when I said I had to get hold of some items for my tool box, I was actually shopping in a drug store."

Peter was the undisputed hero and compliments were lavished upon him by everyone.

Kate and John, despite their jet lag, had no sensation of being tired at all and continued gazing into the carry-cot, mesmerized by their beautiful daughter.

Thirteen

Roberto booked a flight to London for the day of their arrival in Nassau. However, as the flight was not scheduled to depart until 4 p.m., they checked into an hotel at the airport, with twelve hours wait in which to relax.

The flight from Miami, together with the tranquil atmosphere of the Bahamian island, lulled everyone a little from the dramatic and extraordinary events that had occurred in a land across the sea. For John and Kate the sensation of being on British territory gave them a sense of security. The nightmare was over and they could, at last, relax.

Baby Sarah had her own internal alarm clock and at 6 a.m. decided everyone should be up. Kate had finally succumbed at 4:30 a.m. She would have been pleased to spend just a couple more hours alongside her snoring husband, who had had the luxury of sleeping from 3 a.m. However, it was she who had to prepare breakfast for the little noise generator.

From the moment Sarah's mouth detected the warm milk, it was as though a muting button had been pressed. Silence reigned once more. Despite the disturbance Kate was very happy to perform the task and felt she would give up sleep forever in exchange for the joy of holding Sarah in her arms.

John continued to sleep, immune to the pronouncements of his daughter. Kate glanced at him and pondered - would he change, would he give her peace? She had tried so hard to convince him she loved only him, there *were* no other men in her life, or her mind. Jealousy could be flattering, but his fits of rage were potentially dangerous.

For Kate the situation was extraordinary. John loved to paint naked women more than any other subject. In fact it was while she was modelling for him that they first met. Now he would happily lock her away. He could not bear her to even talk to another man and if she smiled he accused her of flirting.

Where was the justice? On the occasion of that first encounter he charmed her to the point where she could resist no longer. She had never before given herself to any man on the first meeting. She should have taken warning then because when the love-making was over, he began, sarcastically, to accuse her of all sorts of ugly things including promiscuity. Sometimes she wondered if he had married her just to take possession of her, but then in every other way he was a wonderful man and a perfect husband. All she could do was to hope and pray that, in time, he would change.

Perhaps John sensed her eyes and mind concentrating on him because suddenly he woke. His eyes met hers and for a moment there was simply a sustained look. Kate felt hypnotized. Then, from previous experience, she recognized in his expression that he was beginning to develop the urge for lovemaking. It was not the time for her. She smiled demurely as she turned away and began walking toward the bathroom. Behind her she heard and felt him arrive, then his hands ripping the nightdress from her body. He spun her around.

"Kate, I love you so much. I promise I will never be rough with you, or shout at you again. From this time on I will be kind and loving. For two weeks I lost you. My mind was at battle with me. I had to overcome the thought of what was happening to you and my jealousy, knowing that other men were touching you and making love to you. The images still haunt me and tear my heart apart, but now we are together and we have our daughter, our beautiful Sarah. I am so relieved, so happy."

He placed his hands on her hips, gently pulled her toward him and kissed her with intense passion while his hands slipped slowly down to her buttocks which he caressed. When his eyes opened from the kiss he caught sight of Sarah, beside them, drinking from the bottle Kate had prepared.

"Kate, you poor darling, you've had no sleep. Come back to bed. Don't worry, I will suppress my desire for you, we have the rest of our lives together. Things are going to be very different. I will care for you, love you, protect you and we will be happy and peaceful."

John's declaration was sweet music in Kate's ears. Maybe there was some hope. They kissed once more and as their lips parted he took her hand, led her to the bed and they lay down together. She began to breath more peacefully with the passing of anxiety. Her mind grew quiet and in a brief period of time sleep overtook them both.

It was around midday when Roberto and Valerie met Peter and Claudia in the dining room.

Roberto interrupted their casual chat.

"My friends, I need to know I have your support. The flight to London today is not direct, it routes via Miami. My suggestion is that we say nothing to John or Kate for the moment, then when the aircraft arrives in Miami we disembark, leaving them to go on to London alone. They will no longer be in danger but in my opinion our work in Florida is not finished. The organization responsible for almost destroying an innocent young family will continue with their evil work. We must stop them. What do you say?"

"For me, you need not ask," Peter replied without hesitation.

"The same for me," Claudia and Valerie completed the accord.

"What do you propose?" Peter went on.

"OK. Thank you all. You know it is strange, somehow I had no doubt, I asked as a matter of formality." Roberto had a very contented look as he continued. "Well, Karl and Erica Schwartz are now suffering, as they deserve to. They were using their money to buy what God denied them. Perhaps if they had been aware of the entire circumstance of what was involved in satisfying their need they would not have encouraged the criminals by buying stolen goods. A basic problem in the world today, even people who consider themselves honest, when offered something very cheap, do not ask from where it came, like an ostrich burying its head in the sand. And so it goes on, the criminals steal and the good people buy."

"Surely our biggest problem is going to be satisfying the police," Peter interrupted. "We are probably sought as fugitives, with kidnapping added to our rap sheets."

"Yesterday afternoon while the rest of you were procuring everything needed for the evening," Roberto went on, "I wrote a detailed account of what had happened, to that point. I sent copies to the police in the village near to the alligator farm, Fort Lauderdale, and the Maresciallo in

Florence. Today we have two stops to make; firstly the apricot house and secondly police headquarters in Fort Lauderdale. I believe that being honest and open is the best policy. Even so I will go alone. You three can wait outside for me. If I am arrested it will be your responsibility to get me out somehow."

"That's odd," Valerie said. "I believe I've just experienced a hot flash. That is, I had a sensation I would imagine resembles the feeling of that postmenstrual phenomenon."

"Me, too."

"Me, too."

Peter and Claudia copied Valerie's statement, looking at one another with surprise on their faces.

"Well, I am serious," Valerie went on.

"So am I."

"So am I." Once more Peter and Claudia endorsed their claims.

"You will not believe this," Roberto said, glancing from one to the other. "I also had the feeling of a wave of heat travelling from my feet to the roots of the hair on my head." He touched his forehead as he spoke. "Look, I'm perspiring."

The other three confirmed they also had beads of sweat on their brows.

They then remembered having experienced a feeling of impending problems the day before. Nothing had happened so far, consequently, they agreed, if it had been some sort of premonition, it was something that was still to occur. The only hope was Valerie but for the moment they had to think about preparing for the journey back to Miami.

The entire group met, as pre-arranged in the hotel foyer, at 1 p.m., and were taken to the airport by taxi to await the flight.

Peter had been to Bermuda on a previous occasion and was well-informed about the economy, politics, agriculture, and the natural resources of the island. He amused and fascinated everyone with his knowledge and the ninety minutes before boarding the aircraft passed very rapidly.

One hour after take-off, and on final approach to Miami, Roberto broke the news to John and Kate that the Quartet intended to leave the aircraft and return to Fort Lauderdale. The decision came as a great surprise and disappointment to them both.

There were emotional goodbyes and promises of continued contact, but as they began to leave the aircraft Claudia realized she had not had the opportunity to speak to Kate concerning her potential cancer problem. She quickly wrote the name and private London telephone number of her friend, a leading authority, and gave it to Kate, saying, "Please, I want you to contact this friend of mine when you arrive. Tell him you spoke to me. In the meantime I will call and tell him to expect to hear from you. This will be your favour to me. Please promise me, Kate?"

"I will, I will, just as soon as we arrive."

As they left the aircraft Valerie and Claudia dried their eyes and Roberto and Peter swallowed with pride, sorrow, and satisfaction. Watching them leave Kate was also tearful and John suppressed the feeling of having Kate just to himself once more, overriding the old way, with a mental correction that there *are* good people in the world whose only desire was to see them together and not to split them. He began to feel quite sorry they were gone.

The Quartet cleared passport control without any problem, much to their surprise. Probably at this time they would not pass through the departure lounge quite so smoothly.

There seemed to be more police about than usual but that was probably because they were noticing them. They made no attempt to try to be inconspicuous, which probably had the effect of *making* them inconspicuous.

The first call would be at the apricot house and they began to drive in that direction. While passing through a set of traffic lights Roberto caught sight of officer Cellini, sitting on his motorcycle at the side of the road. He stopped the car, walked back and the other three watched in amazement as Roberto and Cellini appeared to be having a friendly chat.

After approximately ten minutes he returned to the car with Cellini.

"My friends, officer Cellini will be off duty at 8 this evening. I have asked him to accompany us on a mission which I have not, as yet, outlined to him, nevertheless he has agreed. May I introduce you to Joe Cellini."

Not only was Joe in the dark but also the other three had no idea what Roberto had in mind. They shook hands with the officer and announced their names, following which they agreed to meet in front of the Parrot Jungle at 9 p.m.

That arrangement having been agreed upon, they continued on their way and Joe returned to his motorcycle.

"Let me explain," Roberto began to ease their curiosity. "This evening when we meet up with Joe we will drive to the apricot house together. There we will declare to the Schwartz couple the full details of the kidnapping of Sarah from Florence, how she finally arrived in Florida and our action in returning her to her parents. At that point Karl Schwartz will have the opportunity of requesting that Joe arrest us all. I doubt very much that he would do that because the circumstances of the adoption are clouded in illegalities, added to which, how could he possibly criticize the return of a child to its parents. Before he can even reach a decision we will offer to track down the principal members of the agency that took his money, thereby highlighting his basic problem. The point of having Joe there is to give credence to our intentions."

"We will also have a witness," Peter said. "I think it's a good scheme."

Valerie and Claudia also nodded their approval.

"Fine, let's go for dinner." Roberto concluded the discussion and they drove into downtown Miami Beach where they had dinner.

The meeting with Joe took place as agreed. He was still wearing his uniform, at Roberto's request, as they drove toward the house.

On arrival the Quartet watched as Joe rang the gate bell, then showed his badge to a camera lens beside the bell push. The gates opened, Joe climbed back in his car and beckoned the others to follow him as he drove up to the house.

It was arranged that Joe would go in alone to explain the situation and prepare the Schwartzes for their meeting with Peter, whom they were bound to recognize. The door was opened by a woman approximately thirty years old with black hair and dark skin, probably South American.

Five minutes elapsed before the door opened again and Joe called them to join him. They were led through to a beautiful room lined with white marble, in the center of which stood a magnificent delicately carved fountain. The whole room abounded with tropical flowers and greenery.

As the Quartet entered the room Joe introduced them to Karl Schwartz. Erica was not there.

Peter felt it was his duty to give the details and he explained from the beginning; the kidnapping of the family in Florence, the forced employment of Kate in prostitution and John in drugs. The transference of the baby to the

U.S.A. and the near tragic encounter of the Quartet with David and his associate. Finally, how he had taken the baby from them and returned it to the parents who were once more a united family and back home in their own country.

As Peter finished recounting the story there came the sound of someone clapping, the slow, sharp noise echoing from the marble walls and up into the cathedral ceiling. At first it was difficult to ascertain from where the sound came, due to the confusion of the echo, but as the person applauding entered further and further into the room everyone turned their eyes to a point behind the fountain.

The hearts of each member of the Quartet dropped when they saw David and Dennis come into view. Each held an assault rifle and gave the impression that they would not hesitate to use them.

Joe, in an impetuous act, attempted the quickest draw in the west but David's reaction, together with the advantage of being already drawn, resulted in a single bullet that was accurate and apparently terminated the life of the policeman.

The premonitions and hot flashes they had all experienced were apparently well-founded and there was worse to come.

"That will do for the moment," Schwartz ordered David. "Get the body out of here. I don't want blood all over the Chinese carpet. I will amuse myself with these four for a while. When I am finished you may dispose of them also but *outside* this time."

Before David and Dennis left the room with the body of Joe, David passed his weapon to Schwartz, who handled it with great familiarity.

"So you are the head of the organization," Roberto deduced. "Once a beautiful baby arrived that suited you, you simply took her. The $300,000 was not the cost of Sarah but your entire investment to date."

"Correct. That is very astute of you. It is a pity your talent will now be lost. Unfortunately David was too soft. I will not waste time concerning myself with a painless death for you all. I just need you to be dead."

As he spoke Roberto realized why they had not been picked up at the airport and why Joe did not recognize them. Obviously Schwartz had not reported the incident to the police.

"You may be interested to hear that yesterday evening I was waiting for David and Dennis when you came to the house. They arrived one hour after you left with the baby. We certainly did not expect you back, but now you are here I will need to have details of how much information has been passed to the police. I don't want to have to give up this house unless it is absolutely necessary."

"The police have full details," Roberto replied.

"That, of course, is what I expected you to say. You will not believe it but in approximately fifteen minutes you will certainly tell me the truth."

David and Dennis returned to the room and took up positions on either side of Schwartz.

"Let us begin," Schwartz said, wringing his hands in anticipation as the South American woman arrived pushing a trolley on which were various items that looked medical in character. "Now we can proceed quietly and painlessly or David and Dennis can begin shooting at limbs. Which will it be?"

Roberto stepped forward.

"Just do what you want with me."

"Such bravery. No doubt, the young ladies are very impressed. No, I would prefer to begin with Peter."

No other words were necessary. Peter stepped forward immediately.

"Roberto, you may join Valerie and Claudia. All three of you sit on the couch. I am sure you will find this very interesting."

Roberto and Peter were boiling inside, only the thought of what might happen to the girls prevented them from taking any action.

The South American woman filled a hypodermic from a small bottle and moved toward Peter.

"Concita is from Peru and is very experienced in ancient Peruvian arts with plants and herbs. She will inject you with a drug that will make it impossible for you to lie."

Peter had on a short-sleeved shirt, consequently Concita had only to lift the sleeve a little and proceed with the injection. Peter made no attempt to resist.

"You will begin to feel confused and sleepy in a couple of minutes," Karl explained, "from then on you will answer all my questions accurately."

Claudia and Valerie watched in horror and anticipation what was happening and what certainly lay ahead. There was no obvious way they could possibly extricate themselves from their current situation. In a desperate attempt Valerie took the right hands of both Claudia and Roberto, as she had done three weeks ago in France, while she concentrated all her energy on David.

As Concita withdrew the needle from Peter's arm she dropped the syringe which smashed on contact with the marble. Immediately David let out a scream, dropped his assault rifle, which fired as it hit the floor, shooting Dennis in the stomach. Then he began frantically rubbing his eyes with his fingers.

"I can't see, I can't see, I can't see," he exclaimed in terror.

"You damned fool," Karl shouted at David. "Look what you've done, and you, you stupid woman, your clumsiness caused the problem in the first place." Karl took the weapon from Dennis and told Concita to pick up that of David. He then began shouting angrily again. "Why am I surrounded by idiots? Concita, get these two out of here, take them to the basement." She looked puzzled for a moment, then Karl realized she could not carry them alone. "Come on. help me get Dennis onto this trolley." Concita did as she was told and together they lifted Dennis onto the trolley, then Concita wheeled him away. By then David was kneeling on the floor, moaning,

"I can't see, I can't see, I can't see."

"Shut up, I have enough problems," Karl shouted as he turned the rifle he held, then struck David violently on the side of his head with the butt. The blow was substantial, causing David to keel over. He made no further sound and lay motionless on the floor.

The Quartet was pleased that the balance of power was now much more even, nevertheless the scenes they had witnessed were horrific and Claudia and Valerie were shaking and crying. Roberto whispered to them that they should try to keep quiet, not wishing to antagonize Karl in his present mood. Then Erica entered the room. She and Karl began a heated argument in German which only Peter was able to understand. It was evident she was angry with Karl.

Peter was still standing and began to sway as the injection took effect. Erica noticed what was happening and shouted what appeared to be a command to Karl that he attend to Peter, because Karl took Peter onto his shoulder and helped him to a chair.

Valerie was confident that she had been instrumental in what had happened and decided to continue with her efforts. She searched for Claudia's and Roberto's right hands once more and this time concentrated her energy on Karl, who had just lowered Peter to the chair. He was still in a bent position and gave a cry of pain as he tried to raise himself to the standing position.

Erica's anger increased and she walked across to where Karl remained bent over and kicked him as hard as she could in the backside, presuming that such an action would have the effect of straightening him instantly. It did not. What in fact happened was that Karl fell head first to the marble floor, his head striking that non-flexible surface before he was able to protect himself with his hands. The impact was so severe that everyone heard as bones in his skull cracked. He gave a slight moan, then remained still.

Roberto wasted no time. Before Erica could arm herself, he leaped forward, locked her arm behind her and encircled her neck with his other arm. Claudia and Valerie jumped up and grabbed the two rifles from the floor, then Claudia went across to Peter.

"Peter, how do you feel?"

"Dizzy," he replied truthfully.

Meanwhile Roberto forced Erica across the room to a closet. He thrust her inside, locked the door and threw the key into the fountain. She continued to shout and curse in German until Roberto shouted back that if she did not keep quiet he would shoot through the door. She became instantly silent.

In the meantime Claudia and Valerie had helped Peter onto the sofa and were trying to establish his condition when Concita returned.

"Where is Signora?"

Roberto pointed to the closet and mimicked turning a key. In response, Concita outstretched her arms and staggered toward him mumbling in Spanish, a language near enough to Italian that Roberto and Claudia were able to deduce that she had been under duress for the past six months, threatened that her daughter would die if she failed to do as she was told.

Valerie went across to Concita, put her arm around her and did the best she could to comfort her.

Claudia spoke to Concita in Italian, hoping she would understand, that she wished to have help for Peter. Concita responded in Spanish once more and indicated in sign language that the effect would begin to wear off in twenty minutes.

Before calling the police Roberto decided he should carry out a thorough search of the house, in the hope of finding a record of those involved with the organization. Before commencing the search it would be necessary to ensure that David posed no further danger. Dennis remained motionless on the floor in an ever-increasing pool of blood. Unfortunately for him his injuries were of no importance to the Quartet until Peter recovered.

"You girls stay here with Peter and Concita. I am going to have a quick look around," Roberto instructed as he took the rifle Valerie was holding.

The house was quite extensive but the first place to search was the basement. That was where Concita had been instructed to take Dennis. The wound he had sustained to his abdomen appeared to have been serious and the chances were that by now he would be unconscious or dead.

Roberto found the basement. The door was locked, a fact that gave him the confidence that he did not need to concern himself anymore about Dennis.

From the basement Roberto began to make a tour of the house. The second room he entered was an office with a couple of computers and various other types of office furniture. He looked through the papers on the desk and found there to be several faxes in German from Salzburg in Austria. Roberto then turned his attention to the drawers of the desk. The top drawer had a key in the lock although it was not locked and when Roberto opened it he found a journal listing many addresses: in Austria, Germany, Italy, and the U.S.A.. On top of the desk was an open, empty brief case, into which Roberto began putting the journal, the letters from the top of the desk, then all the computer discs. That having been done he returned to the marble sitting room.

"I think we can safely call the police now," Roberto announced as he returned to the room where Peter was already coming out of his dizzy spell and the girls were looking to see if they could help David in any way. He was still breathing but was in a very bad condition.

Roberto called 911 and stated that there was a dead police officer and two other injured people at the address. He then gathered together his friends and they left, while Concita gave them benediction.

Fourteen

"We need to get back to Europe," Roberto said as he drove once more toward the Miami International Airport. "We've left such a complicated mess behind it would take too long to sort out with the police here. While we are waiting for whatever flight we will be taking, I will send another report on what occurred this evening at the Schwartz house, together with any information on contacts located in the U.S.A. that I can extract from the journal I picked up there."

"Where in Europe?" Peter asked.

"Well, if you're feeling better now, I would like you to have a look at some letters that were on the desk at the Schwartz house. They are from Salzburg and are in German. There are also a couple of addresses in Salzburg highlighted in the journal, suggesting that they are important."

"I'm OK now. Valerie, pass me the briefcase and I will start looking on the way to the airport."

Peter began reading through the letters Roberto had taken from the desk and soon had some comments to make.

"It would appear that Schwartz was getting into something political in Austria. My impression is that it is a Nazi organization, although they are hiding under the umbrella of a travel club. Give me a few more minutes and I will look at one of the discs referred to in one of the letters, if it is amongst those you picked up." Peter looked through the pile of discs as he spoke. "Yes, here it is."

Peter became quite excited at what he was finding and wasn't aware that they had already arrived at the airport.

"Come on, Peter," Claudia gave him a gentle push. "We are here."

"Oh." Peter began loading everything back in the case. "Well, take the briefcase. I will follow on with the lap-top."

"Peter, you can't walk and read information on a small screen like that. Wait until we arrive at a more convenient place."

"You're right, Claudia, but this material is really very interesting. Roberto, before we get any tickets I need five minutes more. The information could determine our ultimate destination."

They walked at a brisk pace, feeling they were drawing near to the end of their journey. Being after midnight there were not many people about to hinder their progress.

"I think we may have to fly to New York," Roberto said. "I doubt we will find a flight to Europe from here at this time of night. Look, you three sit here. I will begin making enquiries and be back in ten minutes, by which time Peter will have a little more detail. Then we can decide finally what we will do and where we will go." Roberto left, while Peter sat with the two girls in a waiting area.

Valerie watched as Roberto strode off toward the departure monitors. He seemed to be walking normally now, much stronger than even a couple of days before. Doctor Fioruccio's advice appeared to have been correct.

Valerie and Claudia remained quiet, to allow Peter to concentrate. It was only a few minutes before he began to relay the information he was extracting from the discs.

"You wouldn't believe where Schwartz was getting his finances for the first two years," Peter's excited statement jolted Valerie and Claudia back to the moment. "He was working as a guard on that border we got to know so well between Bratislava and Vienna. Apparently when Czechoslovak nationals went out of the country they were allowed to take only $5 in foreign currency together with 500 Czech crowns intended for their return. With so little money, no matter where their destination, they were obliged to carry enough petrol for the journey, in jerry cans. Schwartz introduced his own 'transit Austria tax' on the petrol they carried, which always worked out to precisely 500 Czech crowns. Bastard, screwing every last drop of blood out of the poor Czechoslovaks. When he resigned from the Austrian police he had accumulated a small fortune, currency he invested in Czechoslovakia where it earned up to 20 percent interest. With the new political situation he was able to change the previously useless currency for Austrian schillings and that is how he established his business. Can you believe he came to the U.S.A. as a political refugee from Austria!"

Roberto was standing above Peter, listening to the last part of the story and said,

"I presume we will be making our way to Vienna, from what you have been saying."

"Salzburg would be better, but I imagine that's not possible from here."

"Correct. I guessed we would have to go to Austria. Unfortunately there's no flight till 6:20 tomorrow evening. We must get on the road and go north, it's about a five-hour drive to Orlando. If we hang around here maybe the police will begin searching the airport, then we wouldn't get out at all."

Claudia began the drive north while Peter took the lap-top and made a start on entering the details of the previous evening's events. From Fort Lauderdale they turned inland until they reached the less frequented Route 27.

So much had happened they hardly spoke as they sped toward Orlando, each with their individual thoughts and memories. From Peter's point of view it was better that way, allowing him to concentrate.

Around 4 a.m. the car turned east on I 4, by which time the only one not sleeping was Roberto, who had taken over the task of driving from Claudia. After passing the Kissimmee exit, which Roberto remembered well from the twenty-four hours they spent in the house there, the day after their arrival in Florida, there was just a short journey to the airport at Orlando.

In the terminal building Roberto reserved their tickets for the flight leaving at 4:43 that afternoon and arriving in Vienna at 12:20 the following day. In the meantime they checked into a very beautiful hotel in the airport and managed to get some sleep until 2 p.m..

All four had enjoyed Florida. They had seen some interesting sights and the climate was perfect for the beginning of October. Even so there was that nostalgic feeling of going home as they boarded the aircraft.

Peter had completed listing all the details of their time in Florida and had sent disc copies to Fort Lauderdale and Miami Police HQ with an additional copy to the Maresciallo in Florence. They had not had the chance to speak to the ambassador in Bucharest for a few days but he would certainly be aware that his family were safe and back in England.

They all slept for almost the entire journey to London. There they switched to a British carrier for the onward flight to Vienna, where they finally arrived during a severe thunderstorm. From the point of view of weather there was no doubt they were back in Europe, there being a substantial difference in temperature in addition to the very heavy rain.

It was decided they would drive, rather than fly, to Salzburg, giving them more freedom of movement. Having cleared passport control shortly after 1 p.m it would be no problem to reach Salzburg by early evening.

Vienna was miserable, grey and very wet, making crossing the city very frustrating and unpleasant. They reminisced on the day they spent shopping for warm coats in Vienna three weeks previously and wished they had the synthetic furs with them now

The Autobahn was packed with traffic as they began the journey west, causing Roberto to wonder if they would reach Salzburg as quickly as he hoped. The next day would be Sunday and on reconsideration Roberto suggested to the others that perhaps they should spend the next thirtysix hours in Linz. Monday would be more convenient to begin visiting the addresses in the journal, it was agreed. Up to that point the pace had been quite hectic, added to the tension, drama, and excitement. A rest in the ancient city of Mozart and Mahler appealed to everyone.

On arrival in Linz Roberto drove down to the road running alongside the Danube and found a Gasthof that was not particularly elegant but had a certain charm and romantic atmosphere.

The Quartet had been experimenting with vegetarian meals for a couple of weeks but they could not resist the Vienna Schnitzel being served to the adjacent table. Gold Fassel, absolutely the best lager they had ever tasted, was on the menu and provided a fabulous accompaniment to the meal.

The contrast of totally different surroundings and being free from any commitment had the effect of lightening the conversation. Each one enjoyed the company of the other three; however, at 10 p.m. the two couples separated and retired to their individual rooms.

Valerie's arm had improved to the point where she was able to remove the plaster cast and prepare herself to Roberto's pleasure. He was lying on the bed, checking through the copy of the information Peter had sent to the police, while he waited for Valerie to come out of the bathroom. When she finally emerged she stood in the open doorway with the bathroom light behind her, the silhouette effect Roberto had enjoyed so much on the previous occasion. For a woman of twenty-seven her breasts were very firm and she had decided to expose them. However, to create just a little subtlety, she wore black silk panties.

Roberto immediately set aside what he was doing and studied her, from her long auburn hair, cascading over one shoulder and partly covering one breast, on down, with a little imagination as to what was hidden. He extended his hand and smiled.

"My darling Valerie, you are so beautiful. I want to kiss every part of your body."

"In that case, this evening I will lay on the bed, as you did in Pisa." He was standing by the time she arrived beside the bed. "Kiss me first."

It was not necessary to ask again. Roberto had reached a pitch of passion that would not be satisfied without the complete act of love-making. He kissed her so hard and so long it was almost painful, though Valerie did not object and enjoyed feeling his passion grow in a physical expression.

As their lips parted, Roberto lifted her gently on to the bed, removed her panties and began his promised kissing tour of every part of her body, even his hands were not idle. She snuggled into the sheets, lifting her arms above her head and mentally departing the world of fright, danger, sadness, cold, and all the other less than perfect sensations. She was left with just one - absolute joy.

Roberto persisted with his kissing until Valerie became so roused that she could wait no longer. She searched with her hand for the link that would join them internally and pulled him onto her. The thrust sent a quiver of pleasure so magnificent that they both sighed at the wonder of it. Each wanted the peak but neither wanted the passion to end.

He delayed and delayed until finally they both climaxed together with his hands cupping her head and his tongue buried deep in her mouth.

Perfectly relaxed minds and satisfied bodies permitted both to enjoy a deep sleep that extended until 9 a.m.

Claudia and Peter had passed a night very similar to that of Roberto and Valerie and when the four met, the girls, with that woman's instinct, were able to detect the signs in the other couple.

Following breakfast they walked together through the streets of Linz. The city had a certain magic, an atmosphere of history and ghosts of the great musicians who had lived and worked there. The narrow, cobblestone streets of the old city added to each couple's romantic mood and complemented their desire to be happy and, for a short while, depart the world of hate and greed, with which they had been confronted for the past three weeks.

Peter recalled the matter of Schwartz and his deplorable action in taking what was so valuable to the Czech people as they passed through his care. As they continued on their way they passed a middle-aged couple looking in a shop window and speaking a language that certainly was not German. Peter tried,

"Good evening."

The couple turned, smiled and both replied,

"Good evening."

It was not enough for Peter, or the couple who stopped and walked toward the Quartet. They held out their hands and the man spoke.

"My wife and I are from the Czech Republic and I want to tell you how pleased we are to hear the English language."

Peter responded as they shook hands, that they were mixed English and Italian. He mentioned they had been in the Czech and Slovak Republics only a couple of weeks before and that they had a high regard for the people of those two nations.

Soon the group of six were sitting in a beer keller chatting happily and exchanging stories. Peter could not resist raising the question of the relationship between Austria and what was then Czechoslovakia.

The husband declared, "Our peoples have a certain respect for one another but my personal experiences have not been happy and frankly, I don't like Austrians. They were united with the Germans in the last war and since the war are only interested in what they can get from us because everything is so much cheaper for them in our countries."

They had introduced themselves as Waclav and Vlasta. Vlasta reprimanded her husband and said that he should not talk like that.

Waclav continued, unmoved by his wife's caution, and began to tell the story of one occasion when he and his wife decided to make a trip to Linz in 1990. It was extraordinary because he went on to relate exactly the circumstances Peter had read from the Schwartz disc. Peter said nothing but asked if Waclav thought there were still Fascists in Austria.

"I can give you the address of a Gasthof fifty miles north of here where you would not get a room, because you are obviously not German or Austrian, and where the walls are plastered with photographs of Hitler, Goering, and all the other Nazi criminals."

"Please, I would like to know where it is," Peter said, taking a note-book and pen from his pocket.

Waclav wrote the address and cautioned the Quartet not to take any chances. The regime was alive and well.

The conversation continued for several hours and the Quartet were absolutely amazed at what they heard. Waclav had been a professor of political science before he retired and had made a study of the remains of the Nazi party after the war. He tracked its route to its present underground situation.

Roberto invited Waclav and Vlasta to be their guests for dinner. Like Peter, he was very anxious to show them the addresses in the journal.

"Answer me one more question," Peter asked, when he shook hands as they parted. "If you feel that way about Austrians why do you come here to Linz?"

"My greatest passion in life, after my dear Vlasta, is music. Here in Linz I feel very close to the great masters, some magnetism has always attracted me to this city. When I am here the people of today do not interest me, they are just blurred images on the streets."

"It has been a great pleasure meeting you and we look forward to seeing you again at 8 p.m." Roberto said as he shook hands with the old couple, followed by Peter, Valerie, and Claudia.

The Quartet returned to the hotel bubbling with the new contact and feeling sure that Waclav would know something about the addresses in the journal.

There were three hours before their dinner appointment and Peter suggested they should sit together and study the information they had. Since he had not yet had a chance to look at most of the discs, the potential information was intriguing.

Waclav and Vlasta were punctual and soon the group of six were sitting deeply immersed in a conversation over dinner. Having looked at a couple of the discs, Roberto and Peter had decided that the data was too sensitive to be discussed over dinner, where they might be overheard, and during the course of the meal they asked Waclav and Vlasta if they would go with them to Peter's room after dinner so that they might demonstrate what they had. Waclav was very excited when he heard what Peter whispered to him, concerning the source of the material they had, and agreed very enthusiastically with the idea.

The six seated themselves once more in the room where Peter and Claudia were staying and were about to begin the discussion once more when Waclav took a bottle from his jacket pocket.

"My uncle has a cottage in the country and grows plums and apricots. The fruit is very good but even better is the slivovitz he distills from it. I would like to offer you all a taste of that delightful nectar."

"I have heard of slivovitz but have never tasted it," Peter confessed. The same situation applied to the other three.

From another pocket Waclav took a stack of very small glasses and filled each one from the bottle. He passed one to each of the group, then raised his little glass.

"Na zdravi," Waclav's salute as he emptied the contents of his glass in one swallow.

Everyone endeavored to pronounce the obvious toast, then proceeded to attempt to emulate the method of drinking. Before even a teaspoon of the liquid had passed through their mouths they each quickly straightened up and coughed and spluttered as the fiery fluid burnt its track down their throats.

"My God, that's strong," Roberto said with a rather strange, weak voice.

Everyone drew the same conclusion and proceeded much more cautiously from then on.

Peter invited Waclav to look at one of the discs and brought the files up onto the small lap-top screen.

"Just a moment. I must clean my glasses." Waclav removed his glasses, cleaned them with his handkerchief and replaced them. For a moment there was silence, then his face began to light up as he digested the information.

"Where did you get the discs?" he asked Peter.

"We have just arrived from Florida where we had a very serious confrontation with a man called Karl Schwartz."

"You know Karl Schwartz?" Waclav questioned in astonishment.

Peter went on to explain their experiences of the previous week, while Waclav sat flabbergasted and in silence. At the end of the story, Waclav asked whether it would be possible to confirm if Schwartz was dead.

"I doubt it," Peter replied. "We certainly heard the bones cracking in his head when he hit the floor but it was not my impression that he was dead."

"Please show me more of the data."

At 2 a.m. the next morning Peter finally switched off the lap-top and Waclav sat back deep in his chair. He assumed the look of someone who had just seen the world for the first time.

"Do you realize what you have here?" Waclav asked Peter.

"Well, a great deal of it I am seeing for the first time but from what I had seen before I had the feeling it was something very important."

"This information is enough to locate and destroy the final remains of the Nazi party. It is something that has to be done. It would be useless turning it over to the war crimes court. By the time they got around to doing something, the whole organization would just dissolve and regroup. The chances of such a bombshell ever becoming available again are extremely unlikely because they would ensure that such a mistake could not be repeated."

"What do you suggest?" Roberto asked.

"What I am going to tell you now, I would not tell my best friend. I have only known the four of you for six hours and yet I feel I can be perfectly open with you. The fact is that I belong to a very secret society whose aim has been to ensure that the Nazi regime never becomes a dominant power anywhere else or at any time now or in the future. We have been working for fifty years with agents all over the world. The Nazis have a suspicion we exist but have not, as yet, succeeded in tracking us down. You have stumbled across information we have sought throughout our fifty-year existence. That we should meet is a miracle. By the way we are not a Jewish organization. We have representatives in most European countries and there are members whose names I would not repeat in this room."

"You mean political heads of government?" Peter asked.

"Political and industrial," Waclav replied. "The material is in your hands. I would like to ask you to consider passing it over to us. I promise you it is far too big for you to handle. It is not something that can be dealt with through the normal channels of law and order. We are speaking of elements bent on undermining the established society in the world, not just Europe. If they ever have the possibility again the world will see new masters, there will be a total domination. The ordinary people of the world would become subservient to one controlling body of just a handful of men, headed by the major financial kings in the world."

"You say it is too big for us. Is it not too big for anyone?" Roberto asked as he took Valerie's hand.

"Throughout history there have been dictators. They came and went, the forces of right finally prevailing. In today's world the complexities of global trade and politics have made it possible for a cancer to begin growing, unseen by anyone, because the rest of the population are absorbed in their own lives. Throughout the spectrum, from good, honest, God-fearing people to the most organized crime syndicates, all are oblivious to the actions of a select few. There are maybe less than one hundred, slowly but surely establishing themselves in positions where, one day, they will emerge with total control of industry, science, the major political parties etc., etc. The Nazi party, and I don't mean those who are known to the CIA, I mean the Nazi elite, is growing under that umbrella. They will be destroyed by the masters when the time comes, but until that time they will be encouraged to grow once more as they did in the 1930s. Once they emerge they will be supported with such resources that it will be perfectly feasible for a new Nazi-controlled empire to emerge, encompassing the entire globe. At that moment the rug will be pulled away from underneath them and the real master will take control."

"This all sounds so far-fetched," Valerie declared, "that I believe it."

"I know what you mean," Claudia agreed. "Something that appears to be so outrageous no one would even think of it."

"Peter, Valerie, Claudia, I vote that we should hand the information over to Waclav," Roberto proclaimed.

The vote was unanimous and Peter collected together all the information and handed it to Waclav. As he did so he recommended that they swear an agreement never to speak a word of what had been discussed that evening to anyone. It was agreed and because of the late hour the six agreed to meet once more the next day at 11 a.m., at which time Waclav would explain the next moves. The Quartet was entitled to know.

Fifteen

Sunday morning by the Danube was sleepy and no one was in any hurry to leave the warmth of their beds for the continued drizzle of the grey October day in Linz.

Finally at 9 a.m. Claudia opened an eye and saw that Peter was not beside her. She lifted herself on to one elbow and glanced around. There he was, sitting by the table deeply engrossed in his lap-top, as usual.

"What are you doing?" she asked.

"I'm studying the Schwartz data."

"What? But you gave the discs to Waclav last night."

"I did but I had already entered the information into the hard drive of the lap-top."

"Does Waclav know?"

"No, of course not. The point is, if anything should happen to him or the discs, the information would not be lost. I made the copies immediately I realized how important the data was."

"Will you tell Roberto and Valerie?"

"Of course. Listen, the discs contain the entire history of the Nazi party from the end of World War II. I'm surprised how much evidently secret matter was entered without even a security code. They have cells in all major cities of the world, and hold huge blocks of stocks and shares in all the top companies in those cities. The holding companies are bogus, just names registered in Colombia, Liberia, Abu Dabi, etc., etc."

"What do you propose to do with all the information?"

"For the moment I am not sure. Handing it over to MI5 or the CIA, I don't think is the answer. We must discuss it as the Quartet. A decision as important as this will have to be unanimous."

"I'm a little frightened," Claudia confessed. "Don't you think there is a possibility that someone from the organization will, sooner or later, learn or at least suspect that we took the discs?"

"I want you to be peaceful, but it is no use my telling you that I don't think so when I do; however, for the moment the chances are that, as we have arrived this far without being followed, presumably if we were known to be here and had the discs no time would be wasted. They would just come and get them. So for the moment try to keep calm. We will decide what to do when we meet up with Roberto and Valerie later. Hey, look, it's 9:30. Will you be ready in time? We said we would meet Roberto and Valerie at 10 a.m."

"It will be a panic but I will be ready."

Roberto and Valerie were already waiting in the dining room when Peter and Claudia came down for breakfast. Morning greetings were exchanged together with a few jokes about laying in bed too long in the morning.

"I don't think we should speak here," Peter cautioned. "I have some very important things to tell you all. I suggest we go for a short walk after breakfast, now that the rain has stopped."

Not only had the drizzle finally come to an end but there were the first shafts of light from the morning sun breaking through the clouds, picking out small circles of activity and places, like theatre spotlights, as they glanced up and down the tranquil river and across to the rolling hills on the other bank.

There was little time before their appointment with Waclav and Vlasta, so they restricted themselves to black coffee and by 10:30 were walking along the bank of the river while Peter explained what he had found in the Schwartz files. Roberto thought that Peter had been correct in retaining the information in the computer and complimented him on his resourcefulness.

By 11 a.m. they were back at the small hotel. The other couple had not yet arrived so they waited in a small lounge where a television was relaying local news. No one was paying too much attention until Valerie suddenly interrupted their casual conversation.

"Peter, listen, I think they are talking about Waclav."

The conversation stopped instantly and everyone glanced at the TV screen. After a few seconds of news information that only Peter was able to understand, an outside broadcast unit began transmitting live information. A police crew were lifting the body of a man from the Danube. The Quartet suddenly realized that the background to the shot was very near to the hotel.

"Come on," Peter called as he jumped up and ran from the hotel. The other three followed with all haste and joined Peter as he walked toward the river once more.

People were beginning to emerge from the houses in the vicinity and walking in the same direction as Peter. Soon they saw a small group of police and emergency workers being filmed by a TV crew. As they drew close Peter told the others, in subdued tones, that the body of Waclav had been found floating in the river. The newscast stated he had been shot four times. There was no indication as to who had killed him or why. His wife was being questioned.

It soon became clear they would not be permitted to get close to what was going on and Peter called the other three back from the crowd that was forming and quietly said he thought they should get to the car.

No one asked why, they simply turned around and returned to the hotel, Peter leading the way.

Once there Peter asked the hotellier to open the large wooden gate that closed off a small parking area where their car was parked. The girls went to their rooms and collected everything while Roberto paid the account

A few minutes later the car was speeding away from the hotel and the brown Danube.

"Maybe I am overdramatizing," Peter said, "but I think we need to get as far away from here as possible. In fact, I believe we should make our way to the British Embassy in Bratislava. What do you say?"

"I think you're right," Roberto replied, "There is little doubt that, sooner or later, someone will associate us with Waclav, then the police will begin looking for us and the Nazis will also make us their next targets. We will need to take the road back to Vienna; from there we can continue East, cross the Danube to Bratislava and go straight to the British embassy."

They had travelled approximately ten miles from the hotel when Roberto pointed out there was a police car following them. The car had turned onto the road behind them a couple of miles back. "It's no good trying to outrun them," he said.

"What are you going to do, Roberto?" Peter queried.

"Play it by ear, it's all we can do. Here they come." Roberto's nervous announcement was accompanied by the unmistakable sound of a police siren. Everyone looked back and saw the patrol car lights flashing as it increased speed and began to close the gap. Roberto pulled over and waited. The green BMW drew closer and closer but didn't reduce speed and as it flashed by the Quartet realized the police had some other prey in mind.

Everyone breathed a sigh of relief and they continued on their way, reaching the Slovak/Austrian border four hours later. As they passed through the border south of Bratislava, everyone agreed they could imagine the terrible problems the Czechs and Slovaks must have experienced when Schwartz was running his private little racket.

Fortunately they were known at the embassy from their visit there three weeks previously, and the fact that they declined to explain why they needed the protection of the embassy was accepted. They were given accommodation while they established their intentions.

The ambassador in Bucharest owed them a great debt of gratitude and would, consequently, be a better confidant.

Roberto telephoned Bucharest and spoke to the ambassador, who was delighted to hear from them and promised to send his aircraft to pick them up within four hours. He also expressed his sincere gratitude for what they had done in rescuing his family.

It was arranged that an embassy car would take them to the airport in Bratislava. It was only a short journey so they were able to wait in the embassy building, where they felt quite secure, until the call came to say the aircraft had arrived.

When they climbed aboard the Navajo aircraft they were all surprised and very pleased to see the ambassador. He had taken the time to come and meet them and the excuse to pilot the aircraft himself, which was his passion.

Upon arrival in Bucharest they were driven to the embassy and the ambassador made himself available to hear the story they were anxious to relate.

The ambassador was shocked and horrified to hear the details concerning Schwartz, the man who had been holding his grand-daughter only a few days previously.

"It seems to me that one of the major problems is if the organization is so extensive it is difficult to know who one can trust," the ambassador said as he assumed a look of deep thought. "I have a friend of many year's standing. He is, at present, political advisor to MI5. I suggest that I call and urge him to come here. The other possibility would be the international court at the Hague, but I appreciate your concern that the legal authorities are limited in their scope of action, being obliged to act within the bounds of the law, whereas this matter requires hundreds of simultaneous strikes immediately. To seek out and destroy a world network you need another world network with complete freedom of action."

Roberto added that the Israeli secret service have an impeccable record and would certainly be very anxious to eradicate such an organization.

"You mentioned," the ambassador went on, "that Waclav made a point that the secret organization he belonged to was not Jewish in origin. Did he also indicate why that was?"

Roberto replied that he had not, and put forward the proposition that, perhaps, had a Jewish group been involved before, they might have taken action prematurely, before all the information was available, thereby alerting the rest to the danger. The beauty of what they now had was that the information was probably virtually complete in itemizing the names of all those involved. Maybe now would be a good time to contact the Israeli secret service.

"We need to get back to Linz and speak to Vlasta," Peter suggested. "She could perhaps put us in touch with the secret organization Waclav spoke of. Maybe Waclav did not have the opportunity to pass on the information. She would also know the answer to that. However, to return we would need new identities."

"I believe this matter is so urgent that I must act on my own discretion," the ambassador said. "I will organize new passports for each of you. You must realize that you would be entering a very dangerous theatre and if anything happened I would not be able to assist you."

The Quartet realized that that was the case and confirmed their understanding.

"Peter," the ambassador continued, "I have a surprise for you. Please come with me."

There was only one thing the surprise could be and that was his beloved Ferrari. Peter followed as they walked through various corridors, then down a flight of stairs at the foot of which a door led into a garage.

Under a canvas cover was the unmistakable outline of the Ferrari and Peter was overcome with a fatherly feeling, as if he was about to meet a dear son after a long time. He slid the cover off the car and there in gleaming black was his beautiful and much missed treasure. The mechanic he had selected had performed a miracle. The last time Peter had seen it, just about every panel was dented and much of the glass cracked or missing,

Peter lifted the hood and drooled at the sight of the polished engine. He could not resist. With the hood still open he sat himself in the driver's seat, and started the engine. The mechanical parts leapt into action and played a symphony to his ears, that wonderful Ferrari exhaust incited by the action of Peter's foot revving the engine.

"That's music to me," Peter said excitedly.

"I can understand your passion for such a beautiful vehicle," the ambassador confessed. "As you know my delight is my aircraft, but I can appreciate the engineering miracle that is so important to you. I am sure you cannot wait to take it for a spin."

"How right you are, though first I must go for Claudia."

"Go, enjoy yourselves. But tonight if you can tear yourselves away I have arranged a little soiree for you all. Would 8 o'clock be convenient?"

"That would be fine," Peter confirmed as he began to hurry for Claudia. "We will be there."

Peter and Claudia spent the afternoon driving through the streets of the city of Bucharest to the great delight of the local people, while Roberto and Valerie made telephone calls to Italy and Switzerland. All was well at *Il Palazzo*. Roberto spoke to his two aunts, Cecilia and Simonetta, who were very excited to hear from him and assured him there was nothing to worry about. Valerie's mother was back home in Switzerland and relieved to hear from Valerie, who gave her no indication as to the dangerous situations she was involved in.

The following morning Peter made an additional copy of the 'Schwartz' material and it was lodged in a safe at the embassy, in case of emergency.

During the afternoon the political adviser to MI5 arrived from Rome where he had been attending a conference. The ambassador invited the Quartet to join him in the main conference room.

"Roberto, Valerie, Peter, Claudia, it gives me great pleasure to introduce you to Sir Kenneth Donaldson."

The Quartet shook hands with their new acquaintance and there followed a very long discussion with Sir Kenneth, in which the Quartet outlined the entire story.

Sir Kenneth knew of a dossier held by MI5 on activities of the Nazis in Europe but he had no knowledge of the other organization that was using them as a shield.

"The project is finance-oriented," Peter went on to explain. "Have you ever considered that the Federal reserve, for example, has nothing to do with the federal government in Washington? It is in fact a private organization which is indirectly linked to the Bank of England and all other major banks in the world. There is no recorded evidence, nothing that could give rise to concern or investigation. That is the subtlety of the whole plot. From what I have been able to establish from the discs, as much as 70 percent of the world's financial resources are controlled by a small group of financial experts. However their involvement is cleverly concealed under the names of major stockbrokers."

"But surely," Sir Kenneth interrupted, "it would be possible to trace the names of the group through their stock holdings."

"No," Peter continued. "The share certificates are registered in the names of off-shore corporations and spread over such a vast array of companies and names that no pattern would be detectable. In addition to which the majority of the names involved are amongst the most respected in the industry. A surprising number of leading politicians are at the spearhead of the force, although they are being misguided and will eventually be eradicated. The group has almost total control of all communications, via a network of subordinates in places of authority in TV, radio, and the newspaper industry. When I first saw the material such a plot seemed inconceivable to me but the more I digested the more I became convinced that what appeared a mammoth and insurmountable task was surprisingly simple when approached from the top."

The discussion continued for hours, during which time Peter and Roberto explained the bulk of what they had seen and heard. They both felt it very important that Vlasta should be located before any action was taken. There was always the possibility she was involved and may in fact have murdered Waclav and taken the discs. As his wife she had been in a good position to be privy to all information for the previous fifty years.

The major point of concern was that if any operation mounted did not locate all the members almost simultaniously, those remaining would go underground and begin all over again. Sir Kenneth appreciated that and told the Quartet not to concern themselves, MI5 was diverse enough that it would be quite capable of dealing with even a multi-destination operation.

"I see Vlasta." Valerie's voice issued forth the words in that strange tone that indicated, to those who knew her, she was having one of her premonitions. "She is leaving police headquarters in Linz. Now she's in a car with another man and handing him the discs. She spoke his name, Dieter." Then Valerie's tension subsided and it was over.

The ambassador had been obliged to return to his duties but Sir Kenneth saw and heard what happened and was amazed, commenting on how useful Valerie could be to MI5.

"Are you all right?" Roberto asked. He was always a little concerned when she was taken over by the strange force.

"Yes. I'm OK, thank you. Tell me what I said."

Roberto repeated all they had heard.

"There was something else," Valerie said. "When Vlasta said the name Dieter she was not in the car any more, she was standing under a sign, with large letters, U Bahn Wien. I don't know what it meant."

"That's the underground railway system in Vienna." Peter's knowledge of German was once again useful. "It will be much more difficult to find her in Vienna. The advantage to us, however, is that we will be far more inconspicuous there than in Linz."

"I wonder if the Slovak border police could help us trace her?" Roberto conjectured. "There is one way to find out. I think we must begin."

"What you have told me today will go no further until I hear from you again," Sir Kenneth promised. "I will give you my direct number in Rome. I must return there tonight and will be there for four or five days, after that this number in London is my base office." He wrote the numbers on a card and handed it to Roberto.

The Quartet began to plan their return to Austria. Early the next morning Peter and Claudia would leave in the Ferrari, arriving in Vienna during the evening. Valerie and Roberto would take the first available flight to Vienna. Once they were reunited they would make the short journey to the Slovak border, where they hoped they might get information about Vlasta.

Claudia and Peter decided to leave at five in the morning and consequently were obliged to get to bed quite early, while Roberto and Valerie spent the evening in the company of the ambassador and his wife exchanging interesting experiences.

Before retiring to bed, Valerie and Roberto sat together in the beautiful room set aside for them, and confirmed to each other the depth of their love. From first sight they had been destined to be together. It had been a torrid month with so many diverse events, they could be fooled into believing they had been together for years. They confessed they could hardly remember their lives before they met. Gentle kisses that contained a wealth of love closed the day.

Sixteen

Roberto had made reservations at a hotel situated at the airport of Vienna and they were able to walk there from customs and passport clearance. Valerie recalled her arrival there just one month previously, when she met Claudia for the first time, a meeting Claudia also mentioned when she and Peter arrived later the next day.

Now the Quartet was reunited they had a quick coffee then began the drive to Bratislava. From the airport it was only about a one-hour journey, but it was a journey that brought back many frightening memories for both Valerie and Claudia, initiating, as it did, a hunt through several eastern European countries.

On arrival at the Slovak border, just south of the city of Bratislava, Roberto asked to speak with the senior officer at passport control. As they waited they were amazed at the number and variety of private cars towing trailers full of boxes of goods crossing into the Slovak Republic, many vehicles bearing international plates from Poland, Bulgaria, Rumania, etc., etc., an indication of the lively trade being conducted by private individuals inside what were the eastern bloc countries.

"I am Colonel Vlado Kovac," a kindly voice announced. "How may I help you?"

"We are trying to trace a couple we met in Linz, a few days ago," Roberto stated, attempting to sound very casual. "They told us they were from the Czech Republic but as we were near to Bratislava we thought we might begin here."

"What are their names?"

"Vlasta and Waclav Sovicek. They were both in their late 60s."

"Please come to my office. I will enter the details into my computer and see what comes up."

"Thank you, that is very kind of you."

The four had a common thought, while they waited, that maybe they were in the process of entrapping themselves.

"I think I may be able to help you. One week ago a couple with the names you gave passed through the border at Mikulov en route to Vienna. He is 69 and she is 67. Do you have any other information?"

"Waclav told us he had been a professor of political science, although he did not mention the university."

"OK, that confirms that the couple in question are the same couple I have listed. If you wish I can give you their address in Brno. I also have an address in Vienna where they intended to stay for two weeks."

"May we have both addresses, please?"

"Certainly, but I must record your details against the fact that we supplied that information."

Armed with the addresses the Quartet left the border and returned immediately to Vienna, where they located the first address in an apartment block. Peter enquired of the concierge if he knew whether or not Vlasta Sovicek was in the building. Apparently she was out but expected back within the hour.

The news was very promising and they decided to wait. Twenty minutes later a Mercedes drew up in front of the building and Vlasta got out. Valerie noticed that the driver of the car was the same man she had seen in her premonition.

They quickly agreed it would be prudent to follow the car, a task allotted to Peter and Claudia who took off behind the Mercedes, leaving Roberto and Valerie to confront Vlasta.

As Vlasta entered the apartment block, Roberto and Valerie followed her through the main entrance doors.

Roberto called to her, "Vlasta."

On hearing her name she spun around with a very surprised look on her face. "What are you doing here and what do you want with me?"

"Forgive us for startling you," Roberto said apologetically. "We just wanted to tell you how sorry we were to hear what happened to Waclav."

"I don't know what you are talking about," Vlasta replied coldly. "My husband is in the Czech Republic. Nothing has happened to him."

"Oh. We understood there had been an accident. May we come in and speak with you for a couple of moments?"

"That will not be possible. Please leave me alone. Good night." With that unexpected rebuff, Vlasta turned and walked to the lift, closing the gate behind her.

It was clearly useless to think of pursuing the matter, leaving Roberto and Valerie no alternative but to await the return of Peter and Claudia, to see what they had found. There was obviously something very strange going on and Roberto spoke, once more, to the concierge who confirmed he had seen Waclav leaving for the Czech Republic that morning.

When Peter and Claudia arrived they told the other two they had followed the Mercedes to a large house on the southern outskirts of the city. The gate bell had the name Dieter Schroeder indicated, confirming Valerie's vision in which she heard the name Dieter. For the moment that was all. Roberto related the brief conversation with Vlasta and the fact that the concierge had spoken of seeing Waclav earlier that morning.

"We must go to the Czech Republic and find Waclav," Roberto said as he began to leave the building followed by the other three.

It was around midnight when they arrived in Brno, the capital city of Moravia, and began to look for the address. Their first inquiries were unsuccessful, partly because of the difficulty with the language. It was quite late and there were very few people about. Then they met a policeman who spoke German and was able to direct them to a new development alongside the Brno-Prague highway.

Having found the address they decided 1 a.m. was not a good time to ring someone's door bell. They would return in the morning.

Finding an hotel presented its own difficulties and it was after 2 a.m. when they finally walked into the "Myslivna," an hotel used by hunters. There were many visitors from Italy, Germany, and France, taking advantage of the almost complete lack of restrictions on which game could be shot. Not a happy atmosphere for the Quartet, all of whom were animal lovers. However, the restaurant was quite good and the rooms comfortable though the tap water was so polluted it was impossible to take a bath.

Morning arrived with a mixture of sun and frost. After a quick breakfast they made their way back to the building where they hoped to find Waclav.

The door was answered by a young woman who spoke neither English nor German, although apparently she did understand they wished to speak to Waclav because she invited them in.

The apartment was very sparsely furnished and the girls sat on the only two chairs available, while Roberto and Peter stood looking out of the window, all four in curious anticipation.

"Good morning," greeted the cheerful voice of Waclav, "how nice to see you. Excuse me, I am afraid the apartment is not very comfortable. One moment, I will bring a couple more chairs."

Soon they were sitting together with Waclav and relating what they had seen on television in Linz.

"Yes, I know, I heard the story also. The man who was shot was similar in appearance to me and the event prompted Vlasta and me to leave Linz immediately, the coincidence was too great. Now that you have found me so easily I think I should call Vlasta right away. It will be necessary for us go underground."

Roberto came straight to the point and queried the situation regarding the discs. Waclav confirmed he had passed the discs to a senior member of the secret organization and apologized for not having kept the appointment in Linz.

"The important thing is that the discs are safe. What will be the next step?" Roberto asked.

"All I can tell you is that very soon there will be some very dramatic news around the world, although, there are so many important people involved and over such a wide area that the logistics are almost mindboggling. You may rest assured that the matter will be handled efficiently and thanks to you four the most comprehensive bloodless coup in the history of the world will not now take place."

"I must tell you," Roberto went on, "before we came here we called on Vlasta in Vienna. She was not at all friendly."

"Well, I must apologize for her. She was very nervous after what happened in Linz and was merely following my instructions that she should consider everyone, without exception, as suspect. She called me and told me you had been to the apartment. Listen, sometime, I would say within one month, you will be hearing from my superiors. They wish to honor you for your contribution to our cause. For the moment I can tell you no more."

"My friends and I will return to Italy now. We wish you all the best and success in your cause."

They exchanged good-byes and left.

As they returned to the car it was agreed that something was not as it should be and they felt they were probably in danger.

Peter put forward the proposition that the whole thing could have been a set-up. Vlasta and Waclav could actually be part of the same group as Schwartz. Even the murder in Linz could have been a fake. Maybe now Waclav had the discs and was confident the Quartet would keep their mouths shut, they would be safe for a while but it was only a matter of time.

"I would like to know who Schroeder is and where he fits in," Roberto said. "Let's return to Vienna and see what we can find out. I would prefer to be investigating them, rather than the other way around."

Once back in Vienna they called first at the Rathaus. With the name and address of Schroeder and some diplomatic questions, they were able to discover that Schroeder was an official in the Austrian chamber of commerce, which became their next port of call. The office building was impressive and the staff very helpful, as a result of which they were able to ascertain that Schroeder held a very important post, being director of the underground railway system in Vienna (U Bahn Wien).

With the new information they agreed it was sufficient to conclude that Vlasta and maybe even Waclav were from the Schwartz group. The whole matter must now be placed in the hands of MI5.

On their arrival back in Vienna they drove to the house of Schroeder once more. It was 5 p.m. and on the off chance they waited, parked a short distance from the house.

At 8:15 p.m. the Mercedes arrived and Schroeder was seen to go in.

The arrangement was that Peter would call at the house, claiming to be looking for an old college friend by the name of Dieter Schroeder. He had lost the address and all he knew was that he lived on the south side of Vienna. Peter had a very charming manner and would endeavor to gain the confidence of Schroeder. It was a desperate move but all they could think of for the moment.

"So, Peter," Roberto began, "it's up to you now. Good luck and don't ..." at that instant there was a tremendous explosion as the house of Schroeder ripped apart. Broken glass, pieces of stone and brick came raining down over a wide area. The car they were sitting in was hit many times and the back window was smashed. There followed a second explosion, probably a gas main, and flames began to shoot high above the rubble that a couple of minutes before was a house.

For a minute all four were stunned and shocked but fortunately no one was hurt. Without a word Roberto started the engine and drove away at a steady pace, not wishing to attract too much attention. They didn't stop until they were back at the airport. There Peter and Claudia set off in the Ferrari to return to Florence and Roberto and

Valerie had the good fortune to get tickets for a flight that was due to leave in just one hour. The rental car had been left in a regular parking spot. Roberto would call the company and tell them where it was once they were back in Italy.

Six hours later Roberto and Valerie were safely back at *Il Palazzo*, awaiting the arrival of Peter and Claudia. While they waited Roberto called Sir Kenneth, who was still in Rome. When he heard the Quartet was in Florence he said he would delay his return to England and stop off there the following day to discuss the latest developments. Roberto invited him to spend the weekend with them, which he accepted.

When Peter and Claudia arrived they all agreed what a great pleasure it was to be back home and for the first time in several weeks they were able to fully relax and enjoy life. The palace was very quiet, compared with when they left. In a way it suited them better because they needed time to gather their thoughts.

In the past whenever Claudia or Roberto had been absent, there was always Edoardo, with his family, awaiting their return. They both half-expected to meet them at the doors of the palace but quickly remembered that that would never happen again. For both the terrible loss had in some way been compensated for by the very powerful friendship that had developed within the Quartet.

Sir Kenneth's flight arrived on time and when they met he confessed he nurtured a deep love of Florence. The substance of the reason for his visit this time was paramount but when combined with a weekend at an aristocratic house in Florence, had the effect of changing work into pleasure.

The final approach to *Il Palazzo* consisted of the long drive lined with tall slim cyprus trees and the smile on Sir Kenneth's face emphasized his appreciation of the beauty that affected everyone who was confronted with the scene for the first time.

The serious discussion began after an excellent lunch. Roberto was confirmed as spokesman for the Quartet and gave details of the last few days in Vienna and Brno. There was a certain amount of doubt regarding Vlasta and Waclav although the general consensus of opinion was that they were probably both part of the Schwartz organization.

For the Quartet the whole affair was over. John, Kate, and Sarah were together and back in England and they had been instrumental in uncovering an international plot of incomprehensible proportions; as Waclav said it was too big for them to handle.

It would take days to wind down and re-enter the normal daily routine they believed they were longing for, or were they?

Note from the author.

It may not have been noticed that the title page of 'Quartet' bears a phrase, as did 'Visions'.

The final book of the trilogy, 'HRAD', which means castle in the Czech language, completes the quotation, which is given here below in full:

1 **I was born when you kissed me,**
2 **I lived while you loved me,**
3 **I died when you left me.**

The full implication of the statement will only be completely understood when you read the final chapters of Hrad.

For your further entertainment I have completed another book, with the title, 'The Love of My Life', the true story of a young Englishman as he passes through the confusion of discovering love. Then the problems and adventures really begin.

If you would care to be notified as the other books become available, simply send a postcard with your name, address and telephone number to:-

VIKI Books
P.O. Box 1228
Inverness
FL 34451-1228.
U.S.A.

Acknowledgments:

To Helen L. Meachim, an
intelligent, unassuming editor,
for her kindness.

To my good and patient wife.
By my side through all the difficulties
and never complaining.

To Gina DiGiovane, Books-a-Million Ocala FL,
who gave me the first opportunity to market my books.

Herbert Edgar February 1994